A DISTANT MIRROR ANTHOLOGY

A DISTANT MIRROR ANTHOLOGY

Essays From
Rise Grand Island,
the Grand Island Senior High
Alumni Newsletter

MICHAEL W. MONK

SMALL BATCH BOOKS
AMHERST, MASSACHUSETTS

Copyright © 2023 by Michael W. Monk
All rights reserved.

No part of this book may be copied,
transmitted, or reproduced without written permission of the author,
except in the case of brief quotations embodied in critical articles or reviews.

Printed in the United States of America

Cover and interior design by Susan Turner

ISBN: 978-1-951568-33-7
Library of Congress Control Number: 2022923862

493 SOUTH PLEASANT STREET
AMHERST, MASSACHUSETTS 01002
413.230.3943
SMALLBATCHBOOKS.COM

*This book is dedicated to my wonderful family.
I hope these essays and pictures provide some sense of my
life experiences, my values, and what brings me joy.*

*So to all of my family, especially to my wife, Janet;
my children, Susannah and James;
and my grandchildren, Victoria and Leonardo,
this is for you.*

Contents

Introduction   1

December 2015—Sixth-Grade Memorial Day Hijinks in 1961   3

January 2016—The Grand Island Carnegie Library Beckons   11

May 2016—The First-Grade Neighborhood: 317 East 12th Street   17

July 2016—Teach Your Children: My Favorite Teachers, Part 1   23

September 2016—Teach Your Children: My Favorite Teachers, Part 2   29

November 2016—The Fecundity of the Heartland   39

January 2017—The Books of My Youth: Chip Hilton   45

March 2017—May 1, 1957: The May Day Dance on the Green   53

May 2017—Victoria's Tent Rules at Age Six   61

July 2017—Ode to the High School Class of 1967   65

CONTENTS

September 2017—The Glorious First Day of School   75

November 2017—James's "Golden Birthday" in Italy, July 10, 1989   79

January 2018—The Glory of the Bard—William Shakespeare   87

March 2018—The Joy of the Olympics   93

May 2018—Susannah's Boston Marathon and a Trip to Fenway   101

July 2018—Ten (or Fifteen) Favorite Books of All Time   107

September 2018—The Wonderful Books of Beverly Cleary   113

November 2018—Leonardo's Love of Sports: Genetics or Environment?   121

January 2019—Adages I Live By   127

March 2019—Poetry in Motion   133

May 2019—Grade School Crime and Punishment   137

July 2019—Recollections of Mike Parmley, Class of 1967   143

September 2019—About Time   149

November 2019—The Magic of Sports Uniforms   153

January 2020—Christmas Memories   159

March 2020—Equal Treatment of Siblings   165

May 2020—A Day in the Life of COVID Lockdown   169

July 2020—Close Encounters With Celebrities   175

November 2020—Wayne Monk, War Hero   181

January 2021—Fun and Games With Children and Grandchildren   187

March 2021—Elmer Kral, English Teacher Extraordinaire   193

CONTENTS

May 2021—The Sport of Kings: Nebraska Horse Racing   199

July 2021—Victoria's Stuffed Animal Wedding   205

September 2021—Middle School Socializing in 1964   209

November 2021—The Cake in the Face Case   215

January 2022—The Golden Era of Pinball   219

March 2022—"Won't You Let Me Take You on a Sea Cruise?"   225

May 2022—Wonder Woman's Boots   229

Photographs   233

Introduction

In October 2014, my lifelong friend George Ayoub, whom I met in 1954, asked if I would like to do some writing for free. He explained that he was going to be the founding editor of a new alumni newsletter for our high school, Grand Island Senior High, in Grand Island, Nebraska. The newsletter, named *Rise* (after the school song), would be published every other month. George asked me to write a column of memories, school recollections, and pretty much anything I wanted. I quickly agreed. I decided to name my column "A Distant Mirror," since I would often be looking back over many years of memories, some more than fifty years earlier.

    As I began to write these essays, I realized what a blessing this was to me. There are a million stories I wanted to tell, and the newsletter provided a regular deadline by which I would have to complete each piece. My essays, as you will see in this book, include school, family, and personal memories, as well as my modest thoughts on a range of subjects, including literature, the arts, sports, travel, and how one spends a productive and rewarding life.

This book contains each of the columns I have written, beginning in December 2015 and continuing through May 2022. As you will see, as time went by, I focused more and more on recent family and personal activities. The wit and wisdom of my grandchildren frequently became the focus of these essays, but I continued to tell stories from the past that I wanted to record.

When I spoke with Trisha Thompson and Fred Levine, from Small Batch Books, the wonderful publishers of my earlier book, *The Tragedy of Orenthal, Prince of Brentwood*, they suggested I include an array of photographs, most relating to the essays, but some simply to be an anthology of my life experiences. This was a terrific idea, although it took some time to select the photographs, which was no easy task.

I hope these short essays provide some enjoyment for all readers.

—Michael Monk,
Okoboji, Iowa, 2023

December 2015

Sixth-Grade Memorial Day Hijinks in 1961

In the late 1950s and early 1960s, Memorial Day was a major event in Grand Island, Nebraska. Many families would visit the local cemeteries—in my case three generations at once—spend time at the graves of family members, and await the formal ceremonies, which always ended with rifle salutes. In our family, the excitement for the children was to get one of the shell casings that fell to the ground after the rifles were fired.

Memorial Day was also honored with festivities and speeches at Howard Elementary School. In 1961, Howard School was a relatively new, simply beautiful school, with a wonderful layout and gorgeous amenities. It seemed normal to those of us who attended. What follows is my recollection of the 1961 Memorial Day convocation.

Chapter 1

While the rest of the students at Howard Elementary School proceeded at their usual pace—some rooms buzzing with activity and some quiet with concentration—sixth graders Julia Dunham, Peggy Burger, and I walked quietly down the halls together toward the building's foyer. The giggling, pinching, and teasing normally observed among grade school children were noticeably absent. There were several reasons for the reserved demeanor. First, the three of us were in the oldest class at Howard, composed mostly of eleven- and twelve-year-olds. In addition, we were definitely on the more studious, "goody-goody" end of the sixth-grade spectrum. But our serious and even nervous manner was primarily due to the gravity of our mission. The three of us were the finalists among all sixth graders for the honor of delivering the "I Am an American" speech, traditionally part of the school's Memorial Day convocation, in front of the entire school, parents, military representatives, and other guests. This day we were each to audition by reading the speech to the three sixth-grade teachers, Mrs. Severson, Mrs. Weidner, and Mrs. Walker, who would then select the winner.

Despite the nervous tension, we each could not resist looking in the other classrooms as we passed them by. Inside, we saw different teachers, students, wall decorations, and the ultimately different realities of each classroom's little world.

As we approached the foyer, where the school gathered for Christmas caroling and other major events, we saw two other sixth graders, Steve Schroeder and Mike Parmley, who were similarly liberated from their classroom and, apparently, enjoying it much more. As the two boys passed the door of the last classroom before the foyer, they walked properly and noiselessly. Once past the door, they began laughing and throwing bits of rubber eraser at each other. They were dressed in blue jeans, "Schro" with a plain white T-shirt and "Parm" with a blue cotton short-sleeve shirt. Parm and Schro both carried cases containing their cornets, which they had begun playing almost two years previously, at the start of fifth grade.

At the sight of my two friends, I carefully whispered, "Schro, Parm, what are you doing out of class?"

"We're playing taps for the Memorial Day deal," Parm said. Julia and Peggy both said nothing but looked reproachfully at the two boys.

Just then a group of teachers approached us, and we three auditioning students quickly proceeded to the front of the foyer, while the two boys with their horns went outside with the band teacher. Parm and Schro were selected to play taps during the final climactic portion of the oration, to provide the solemn and poignant background appropriate for the speech on patriotism and devotion to country. In fact, as the three potential orators were set to begin their auditions, the sound of taps could be faintly heard outside. The teachers remarked on the nice effect of playing the horns out of sight, so the audience hearing them would be both surprised by the horns and moved by the faint sounds seemingly coming from nowhere.

Mrs. Moore, the gray-haired principal, proceeded to organize the audition for the oration. She first asked Peggy Burger to take her place behind the podium, and then she directed Julia and me to be seated in the front row of folding chairs assembled in the foyer in anticipation for the Memorial Day ceremony. The three sixth-grade teachers were already seated in the front row.

I listened closely as Peggy Burger read through the prepared text, and I carefully considered my chances of being chosen to deliver the speech. Peggy, of course, read the text well, but her body movement and hand gestures seemed a little forced, or fake, to me. My views on what constituted a good speech were clearly in the formative stages. I sensed that some emotion was good, but too much seemed silly. I knew that sometimes you should speak fast and with emphasis, and that sometimes you should use pauses, but when to use these techniques seemed pretty much a matter of personal taste to me.

I was the second speaker to try out, and I steadied quickly after a bit of unexpected nervousness at the beginning. I proceeded with a speech filled with emotion. I thought I had demonstrated a nicely balanced use of different speeds of speech and had exhibited good eye contact with the sparse audience. After glancing quickly at the response of the teachers to my effort, I lowered my eyes and walked briskly to my seat. I thought that I had a real shot at the speech, and I thrilled inwardly at the expectation.

When Julia Dunham began her audition, I at first dismissed her as any real threat, since she had only recently begun to gain confidence in her public speaking. But as she continued on, I was immediately struck by her forceful speaking style and her more measured approach. She proceeded gracefully and smoothly through the speech, and at the end she reached a more impassioned pitch than either Peggy or I had been able to do. As Julia concluded, smiled shyly, and left the podium, I sensed I had finished second. After a brief private chat among the three teachers and Mrs. Moore, Mrs. Moore stepped over to us three twelve-year-olds and announced, "Each of you read a simply splendid speech, and each of you would do a fine job if chosen. The teachers and I, however, have chosen Julia to present the Memorial Day speech since her talk seemed particularly to capture the patriotic feeling associated with this event. And I have a special surprise for everyone: A representative of the Veterans of Foreign Wars has agreed to join us and also say a few words."

I grimaced inwardly and a bit outwardly, too, but then congratulated Julia and returned with the two girls to our classrooms.

Chapter 2

The disappointment I felt in being passed over for the Memorial Day speech again arose on the actual day of the Memorial Day ceremonies at Howard Elementary School. Parents, brothers and sisters, and even some grandparents filled the foyer, seated for the most part in folding chairs. In addition, the entire student body of approximately three hundred students was assembled on the floor of the foyer, seated cross-legged in front of the adults in the folding chairs. The air was filled with the reserved excitement of a serious event. Even the youngest children, the five-year-old kindergartners, had been told of the serious nature of gathering, the remembrance of those who died for America. So the presence of so many people and relatives inevitably provided a subdued but festive atmosphere. I would have loved to have given the speech amidst all this excitement. While I considered myself relatively sophisticated with regard to patriotic fervor, on that day I strongly felt the emotion and meaning of the event.

The selection of Steve Schroeder and Mike Parmley to play taps at the climax of the event was a puzzling one at best. Admittedly, Schro and Parm were among the better cornet players at the school, and their version of taps, with harmony, was a good one. Nevertheless, the Parm and Schro combination had all too frequently spelled disaster in the past. In the second grade, the two of them were sent down to the kindergarten classroom by Miss Langdon (later Mrs. Martin when, midyear, she got married) because they were "acting like kindergartners." In fifth grade Parm and Schro had both grown fond of Pamela Cramer, and to best show their affection, they decided to draw a picture of her that was, to put it mildly, inappropriate, and give it to her. Pamela then gave the picture to her teacher, and the principal, Mrs. Moore, had to investigate. After berating the two boys for some time, she pronounced a sentence even more painful than Parm or Schro had imagined. She declared that the two of them could not walk to school together and could not walk home from school together. In fact, to ensure compliance, Mrs. Moore announced that Miss Langdon herself would drive Parm the five short blocks from school to his house on Pine Street.

Notwithstanding this history of problems together, it was Parm and Schro who were stationed outside the school listening carefully as Mrs. Walker, their sixth-grade teacher, gave them the final instructions about playing taps.

"Very well, Mike and Steve, you must wait here quietly while Julia gives her speech. You must not talk or make noise of any kind. After Julia finishes, the gentleman from the Veterans of Foreign Wars will make his speech. When he is almost done, you will begin to play taps. I will step outside the door and wave to you, and at that precise time you should begin to play. Remember, play slowly and don't rush. You should play loud enough to be heard, but softly enough for the mood of the ceremony. Do you understand?"

"Yes, Mrs. Walker," said Schro, who had likely heard little of what she had said, even though he looked earnestly at his teacher while she spoke.

"Okay, Mrs. Walker," said Parm, looking, as he spoke, at a few late arriving parents who were hustling into the school foyer to see the program.

Once Parm and Schro were told to be quiet during the bulk of the ceremony, they immediately were seized by a strong desire to make some noise or, perhaps more accurately, were struck by the impossibility of remaining quiet under the circumstances. The combination of the command to be quiet and the solemnity of the occasion was to Parm and Schro an unspoken challenge. They would defy the instructions willingly, if only to discover just what the consequences would be. This ceremony was a special one, however, and both boys overcame their initial urge to test the circumstances and became silent.

As the ceremony proceeded inside, the boys became restless, however, and each time they would catch each other's eye they would start to laugh and then have to stifle the noise. It quickly became a game of trying not to look at each other and bursting out into audible giggles when they did look at each other.

"No," said Parm to Schro, "don't make me laugh."

"Don't *you* make me laugh," responded Schro, and as the boys looked at each other, they both broke into giggles.

Inside, Julia Dunham was just finishing her oration, and applause rang out in the foyer. Sitting with my sixth-grade class, I thought that Julia's speech wasn't quite as good as I had remembered it at the tryout a few days before. Maybe I would have been the better choice after all. As the representative of the Veterans of Foreign Wars began to speak, however, I forgot Julia's speech and began to become engrossed in the veteran's speech.

The bearded speaker, a gentle man of perhaps sixty years, built toward his patriotically sentimental conclusion. Mrs. Walker quietly walked toward the door at the back of the foyer and looked around to signal to the boys to begin their cornets. She saw them standing in their appointed place, but they were so engrossed in giggles that she couldn't get their attention. She began to wave her arm wildly.

"Parm!" cried Schro. "There's Mrs. Walker."

"Geez, we better get going," said Parm, and they raised their instruments to their lips. The immediacy of the moment, however, struck them both as hilarious, and they burst into laughter, which, with their cornets positioned at their mouths, produced a bleating sound, part laughter and part brass instrument.

Then they recovered to be able to play the initial notes of taps, "*Blah, blah blah . . . ,*" but then the laughter returned, "*blahahahahaha blah,*" and then "*blah ha ha ha ha hu*" was heard within the auditorium. Inside, I immediately sensed that my friends Parm and Schro were somehow messing up their parts and messing up the mood of the ceremony. Once my patriotic flow was broken, however, I felt a smile come to my lips. I then heard the sound of taps, however halting and uncertain, but then immediately I again heard the bleating sound.

"*Blah, blah, ha ha ha ha ha . . . blahahaha . . . blaaahaaahaah.*"

Outside, Parm and Schro were in that delicious yet terrifying limbo created by having done something outrageously bad. After the first outburst, they had momentarily regained their composure, only to relapse into further gales of uncontrollable laughter. Now all was lost. The laughter they had not been able to contain was still within them, but it was being quickly tempered by the enormity of the punishment they knew they would soon face. Mrs. Walker and Mrs. Moore quickly marched out to deal with them, with the sternest of demeanors. I will leave the details of that encounter to the imagination of the reader.

Inside, the mannerly Midwestern audience was confused. The speech by the Veterans of Foreign Wars gentleman had been good enough to carry through the disruption caused by the unusual rendition of taps. But everyone sensed that things had not gone quite as planned. Some students were giggling, some were asking what had happened, and some didn't much care. The parents and families, too, were confused. Some were upset, some were amused, and many simply departed and proceeded about their business with an uncertain understanding of the bleating they had heard.

January 2016

The Grand Island Carnegie Library Beckons

In the 1950s and 1960s, long before Amazon, Barnes & Noble, and eBay, the typical Grand Island student found his or her books at the Grand Island Carnegie Library. It was a badge of maturity and grown-up status to have that most precious item, the library card.

This was also long before the days of iPads, smartphones, PlayStation, and Xbox. Those with a passion for watching sports generally watched the local teams, since often only one Major League Baseball game or pro football game would be shown on television each week. So, when not out riding bikes, playing sandlot baseball, or building forts in the backyard, many grade-schoolers actually read books.

I owe a great deal to my childhood friend and Howard School

classmate Steve Schroeder. Beginning in the second and third grades, he had a profound influence on me. Steve's father was the minister of the Lutheran church on Seventh and North Locust Streets. I would ride my bike to his house to play. Sometimes we would play Wiffle ball outside, but often we would hang out in his basement. The Schroeder family had a wonderful new set of encyclopedias, and Steve would amuse himself by making lists. He started with lists of sports achievements. He would carefully make numbered lists of the top ten home run hitters in baseball history, the top ten pitchers in career wins, the teams with the most World Series wins, and a multitude of other sporting statistics. But he also delved into matters in which I suspect few third graders had an interest, compiling lists, for example, of the top ten iron ore–producing countries in the world, the top ten banana-producing countries in the world, and the ten highest mountains in the world. He opened many doors to me at this early age that would otherwise not have been opened until much later.

By the summer after the fourth grade, Steve and I would make trips on our bikes together to the Grand Island Carnegie Library to check out books. The library, located at 321 West Second Street, at the corner of Walnut and Second Streets, was a beautiful and imposing building. One of fifty-eight public libraries in Nebraska funded by Andrew Carnegie, it was dedicated in 1907, but more about that later.

The books for students in grade school were located in the basement of the building, reached by walking to the entrance on the right side of the library and down the steps. The upper floors held the more imposing and massive stacks of books for adults. The head librarian, beginning in 1960, was Roberta Lawrey, a lady whom I recall being a bit stern but kindly. Far more than today, the code of silence was assiduously followed. But silence was not always possible, in part since the metal stairs were quite noisy, no matter how carefully one climbed them. The basement area had an academic feel and smell to it, with small shelves holding the books and smaller tables and chairs available for reading or studying.

At that time, a library card would permit you to check out a maximum of six books at one time. That summer, Steve and I fell into a routine. We would check out the maximum six books at a time, then go home and dive into them with real zest. Each was proud to announce to the other that he had finished the six books and ask if it was time to go back for more. At first the books I selected were not terribly diverse and would include mostly biographies of my sports heroes. A typical set of six for me might include *The Mickey Mantle Story*, *The Babe Ruth Story*, *The Willie Mays Story*, *The Henry Aaron Story*, *The Ted Williams Story*, and maybe one Beverly Cleary book, like *Henry and Ribsy*. Steve was more adventurous, getting stories like *Freddy and the Men From Mars* and other fantasy books. I eventually branched out to *Tom Sawyer*, *Huckleberry Finn*, other American classics, and lots of fiction about sports.

Another strict rule was that one could never, ever, no matter what, write in a book. To defile a book was among the highest sins. The dignity of the printed word should never be defaced. I accepted this maxim with general agreement, but when I got to college, all that changed. By then students bought their own books and wrote in them liberally, recording thoughts, questions, and emphasizing points the author had made. I today cannot imagine *not* writing in my books. But rules are naturally different for one's private property than for public property. Whoever next read *Freddy and the Men From Mars* would not be interested in Steve Schroeder's scribbled notes.

In a stroke of brilliance, during the summer after my fifth-grade year, in anticipation of the upcoming 1960 Rome Olympics, the city grade schools and the Carnegie Library established a Reading Decathlon. For every ten books a student read that summer, the student would be deemed to have won one of the ten events in the decathlon. This knocked me out. To combine my growing love for reading with the Olympics, in which I was totally engrossed, was magical. So I set out to read my way to winning as many events as possible. That summer I read forty-nine books, winning four events in the Reading Decathlon. But then my family went off on vacation, cutting short my efforts. To this day I regret not finishing just one more book so I could have gotten that fifth event win. When school resumed the next year, there was a ceremony at Howard School to present the awards. I thought I might be among the readers with the highest number of books read, and indeed I was. But to my surprise, there were six or seven students who had surpassed my forty-nine books. I think one student read more than seventy-five books. The Carnegie Library was our friend.

When I grew a bit older, I discovered the magazine section of the library, on the first floor. It of course had magazines with which I was familiar, like *Life, Look, Time, The Saturday Evening Post,* and *Sports Illustrated.* But it also had magical magazines I had never seen, like *The New Yorker, The Atlantic Monthly,* and *The New Republic.*

Many years later, during the Christmas break in my first year in law school in 1971, I would again retreat to the library. It was the one place I could be protected from the disruptions and temptations of socializing with friends, to study for my torts final that would occur when I returned to Philadelphia after Christmas vacation.

Completely unbeknownst to me until I prepared this recollection was the rich history behind the groundbreaking and dedication ceremonies held for the Carnegie Library. Much of this history pops up when one Googles the Grand Island Carnegie Library on the internet. There is a particularly nice piece written in 1984 by Roberta Lawrey herself. Plans for a new library had commenced in 1902. Andrew Carnegie was contacted for the purpose of obtaining funds for a community library building. Carnegie grants stipulated that a city would have to make a commitment to provide ongoing support for the library, as well as provide a site for the building. The board and city council adopted a resolution that the city would provide for an annual levy of $2,000 for library maintenance. G. H.

Thummel, R. R. Horth, James Cleary, and H. H. Glover donated a site at Walnut and Second Streets. Andrew Carnegie then granted $20,000 for the structure.

The groundbreaking ceremony was held on April 27, 1903. By chance, President Theodore Roosevelt was on the campaign trail, taking a cross-country train trip, and he was to have a stop in Grand Island. Mayor James Cleary asked President Roosevelt to assist in the groundbreaking ceremony for the new library. As Ms. Lawrey's story relates, Roosevelt accepted with alacrity and broke the sod with such zeal, Mayor Cleary had to employ agile feet to avoid being a target. A lady in the audience remarked, "He handles the spade better by a whole lot than my spouse."

The Grand Island Carnegie Library was formally dedicated in 1907. Charles F. Bentley introduced the featured speaker at the dedication, William Jennings Bryan. Bryan was another legendary political figure, a dominant force in the populist wing of the Democratic Party. He not only represented Nebraska in Washington as a member of the House of Representatives, but also was selected three times as the Democratic Party's candidate for president of the United States (1896, 1900, and 1908).

By the early 1970s, the community decided a new library was needed. Amazingly, Emil Roeser and Ret. General Theodore Buechler, both of whom had been present at the Carnegie Library groundbreaking in 1903, assisted with the groundbreaking ceremonies in November 1972. The "Roosevelt" spade was activated for this occasion. April 28, 1973, was the date for the laying of the cornerstone. The wonderful and imposing Carnegie Library building, beset by roof leaks and pigeon problems during periods of its history, was then sold to private interests.

While modern libraries contain a wealth not only of books, but also of computer and other resources, I wonder if grade school students today read as much as they did in the 1950s and 1960s. It is, of course, a different world. And while the Grand Island Carnegie

Library no longer exists, the memories it produced and the literary foundation it permitted us to build are still vividly reflected in this Distant Mirror.

May 2016

The First-Grade Neighborhood: 317 East 12th Street

Before this alumni newsletter thing gets too far down the road, it seems wise to be more forthright about my lifelong friendship with Scrooge himself, my buddy George Ayoub. When George includes his and my efforts in the newsletter under the heading "A Couple of Guys From the Neighborhood," he is being neither euphemistic nor inaccurate. So let's take a trip in Sherman and Mr. Peabody's "Wayback" machine to 1956.

In the lively Ayoub house on 10th Street, Monica Ayoub was making popcorn. She dumped the freshly popped corn into a large bowl and brought it from the kitchen into the living room to her younger brother George and his friend Mike Monk. As she strode into the living room, a few kernels popped and flew around the room. Mike and George, both six years old, were in hysterics.

Mike's family moved to Grand Island halfway through Mike's kindergarten year in early 1955. They rented a house at 317 East 12th Street. Mike lived with his grandparents; his mother; his sister Pat; two aunts; and his cousin Randy. George lived two blocks away on 10th Street, and he and Mike immediately became fast friends. They were also best buddies with Bob McFarland, who lived on 11th Street, midway between George and Mike.

Indeed, the entire Ayoub and McFarland families embraced Mike's family and accepted him immediately into their homes. George's mother, Agnes, was a kindly aunt to Mike. She would encourage him, and his success, as much as she did George's. She would not be afraid to keep Mike in line, either, knowing his mother and grandmother would approve. No one was a stranger in the Ayoub house, but all were treated like members of the family. They played endless Monopoly games and, of course, talked sports. George's sister Monica taught Mike how to hit a baseball. A few years later, George and Mike would practice their shot put form in George's backyard with the eight-pound shot put Mike bought at Russell's Sports.

All the kids went to Howard School, and Mike's transition there was very smooth, in part since he had already learned to read in the kindergarten class in the small town of Amherst, Nebraska. At Howard, reading was first taught in first grade.

There was a very embarrassing moment in Ms. Cortes's kindergarten class when Mike had been waiting to go to the bathroom. The child in the bathroom was taking forever. Mike was in pain. Then, after what seemed like hours, the bathroom hog emerged, and Mike relaxed, only to see another student rush into the bathroom before he could get to it. Mike's new light blue denim jeans became dark blue around the crotch, and Mike was allowed to go home for the day. But miraculously, this moment was instantly forgotten, and Mike thankfully was not thereafter known as the "pee in his pants" boy.

The three boys bonded primarily due to a common passion for sports. Well before Little League age, they regularly played baseball in the street on 11th Street, often just the three of them, with a pitcher, a batter, and a fielder. They dreamed about becoming Major League Baseball players and idolized Mickey Mantle, Willie Mays, and Ted Williams. Mike's cousin Randy Garroutte, three years younger, later became a Yogi Berra man himself. In their young minds, playing Major League Baseball was a realistic possibility. Indeed, it was through batting averages that Mike learned how to calculate an average. One day he was stunned to see Mickey Mantle's batting average had gone down. Hits, home runs, and steals never went down, so how could a batting average?

In second grade, with the assistance of Miss Langdon (who later became Mrs. Martin, when she married midway through second grade), Mike composed the following poem, which was published in the *Independent* along with the poems of other Howard School students:

I'd like to be a baseball player,
On the New York Yankees team.
And when I'd hit a home run,
I'd light up like a beam.

As George, Mike, and Bob entered into Little League Baseball at age nine, Bob declared, "Well, now that we are on teams, we can't just be playing in the streets." Mike was totally panicked, saying, "No, we can still play for fun! What are you talking about?" The fear was short-lived, however, since the neighborhood boys continued to play pickup baseball at Howard School, generally organized by Roger Dold, well into their early teens.

The boys were truly raised by a village. When Mike's prized baseball card collection (a virtually complete 1957 Topps set of cards) was stolen, at age eight, George's mother, Agnes, headed up a campaign to try to find the culprit. She even contacted the local radio station, KRGI, to get the message out about this heinous crime. Agnes and George's father, George, along with Mike's mother, Ramona, and his grandmother Doris, were fixtures at every baseball game, basketball game, football game, and track meet in which George and Mike participated. Years later, in 1978, when Mike's mother passed away at age forty-seven, Agnes comforted him at the services, explaining that such a loss would not get better in a week, or a month, or even a year, but that it would eventually get better. When the village works, it is wonderful.

Later on, hundreds of Grand Island students got to know Agnes Ayoub when she worked at Walnut Junior High School. She was that loving friend in the office, always lending a helping hand, and a staunch defender of the important values of honesty, hard work, and need for husbandry of one's resources.

For George and Mike, the days in the neighborhood were a prelude to a wonderful run of experiences in sports at Walnut Junior High and Grand Island Senior High. They were teammates in football, basketball, and track at both Walnut and Senior. They played on the same Little Bigger League Baseball team, the Nats, that won the championship when Mike was fourteen and George was thirteen. Indeed, in the championship game, George's single up the middle drove Mike home from second base with the walk-off winning run.

Mike peaked athletically in junior high school. He played varsity in all sports in high school, albeit at a modest skill level. George, on the other hand, was a total star at all levels of athletics. In North Side Little League Baseball, he was a legend. George was so fast and big that he developed this technique when on base: After a pitch was thrown, he would take a ridiculously big lead, then if a throw occurred to pick him off, he would simply outrun the relay to the next base. It revolutionized Little League at that point. Later, he was a true athletic star in high school. Like the legendary John Sanders, whom Mike and George idolized,

George was a varsity star in football, basketball, and track even in his sophomore year.

Once when George, his wife, Jackie, and their son, Max, were visiting Mike in California in the 1990s, Mike showed Max his high school scrapbook that reflected massive glory for George. Max somehow still couldn't believe it. As the proverb goes, "You are never a prophet in your own land." This history is not to flatter George, or to exaggerate his success, but to clarify a reality that George is too modest to discuss.

But the strongest common bond between George and Mike was, and is, a respect for the traditional Midwestern values: honesty, loyalty, and responsibility. George's father and mother were superb role models for these values.

But to end this brief history, on one occasion the Ayoub family did bring great angst to Mike. George and Mike were lifelong Yankee fans and gloried in their success. Then one day, George's mother, Agnes, told Mike that the Ayoub family actually owned the Yankees. Agnes explained that since the Ayoubs were members of the Knights of Columbus, and since that organization had some investment in the Yankees, they were owners of the Yankees. For whatever reason, Mike was furious! How could George own the Yankees when Mike was just as fervent a Yankee fan? Looking back now, Mike wonders why he wasn't happy with the idea that his friend owned the Yankees. But for some reason it seemed unfair to Mike, maybe because he sensed it was a ruse to annoy him.

Thousands who grew up in Grand Island have poignant and wonderful histories. One suspects that even in today's modern world, many recent GIHS alums have similar stories of the blessings of growing up in a wonderful Midwestern town and going through the Grand Island Public Schools system. So this story is not unique. It is just one of the stories reflected in the Distant Mirror.

July 2016

Teach Your Children: My Favorite Teachers, Part I

Let us today peer into the Distant Mirror to take a look back at some of the teachers who influenced, impressed, or annoyed some of us in the GIPS system from 1955 to 1967. I start by openly professing my love and respect for teachers. I married a teacher, and this August we will celebrate forty-two years of marriage. My daughter taught third grade for a year before leaving this honest work and becoming a lawyer. And I have taught both law school and college courses on labor law.

But most emotionally, when I danced with my daughter at her wedding, the song we selected was Crosby, Stills, Nash & Young's "Teach Your Children." As I look into the Distant Mirror, I am struck by just how many great teachers I was blessed with in the GIPS system from 1955 to 1967. Virtually every teacher I had, whether at Howard, Walnut, or GISH, took teaching seriously and was sincerely interested in the subject he or she taught. I cannot begin to discuss every terrific teacher I had, so this will by definition be a truncated discussion.

I vividly remember each Howard School teacher without prompting, from kindergarten to sixth grade: Mrs. Cordes, Mrs. Dvorek, Miss Langdon, Mrs. Gaines, Miss Lee, Mrs. Severson, and Mrs. Weidner. They were, as a whole, kindly, demanding, wise, and charming.

Miss Langdon (second grade): She was the type who every second-grade boy loved. She was young, nice, and pretty, and I felt completely comfortable with her. I was perhaps too comfortable, since one day when my reading group read about a snowy winter scene, I was bold enough to try some humor. When asked the weather in the story, I smiled and said, "It was bright and hot and sunny." Luckily, Miss Langdon knew I was joking and gently directed me back to the facts, with only the hint of a reprimand. It was, I believe, in Miss Langdon's class that one day Lynn Weiser shouted out, "There ain't no Santa Claus." The room fell silent as the second graders digested this bold proclamation. I was taken aback, but I immediately thought, "You know, I have been wondering about that."

Miss Lee (fourth grade): This tiny little pepper pot was a charmer but a taskmaster. She was often only barely taller than some of her fourth graders, but a superb teacher.

Mrs. Lydia Severson (fifth grade): I also adored Mrs. Severson and her fifth-grade class. My 1967 classmate and friend Gloria Dolton recently shared with me that it was Lydia who inspired her to be a teacher. Each day, after lunch, for maybe twenty minutes, she would read to the class. She chose some great works of literature, including *Black Beauty*, *Johnny Tremain*, and *Robinson Crusoe*. Thirty students, after running around on the playground, came into class, often breathlessly. But the reading calmed everyone down, relaxing and mesmerizing the whole class. I know this engendered a real love of reading for many of us. During milk lunch break, as we called it, she also held a *Jeopardy!*-type competition to name the state capitals. The many competitive students in the class soon learned them all.

I recall only a single moment of anger in her classroom, when an ill-advised "fruit roll," supposedly a gesture of generosity and kindness to the teacher, went awry. One miscreant, who will remain nameless, threw, rather than rolled, a medium-sized watermelon that split open upon hitting the floor, creating a major mess. But this was a rare departure from the happy and kindly tone of the classroom. On the last day of fifth grade, she became serious, saying she wanted to end the year with this thought: "Don't take things too seriously. Life is just a bowl of cherries!" I was taken aback, since it seemed a bit flippant given the seriousness of her approach to learning throughout the year. But I have never forgotten it.

Mr. Epp (seventh grade): The jump to Walnut brought us into a world where we had more than a single teacher; though in seventh grade, the same teacher—a "block" teacher—would teach English, history, and health. This provided a modicum of continuity in the transition from a single teacher. My block teacher was Mr. Epp. He was my first male teacher, and he was both nurturing and demanding. The English instruction was first-rate, and as my late father-in-law would have said, "We diagrammed the hell out of a million sentences." But it worked. We knew an adverb from an adjective.

Mr. Broz (eighth grade): The avuncular Mr. Broz was my charming yet somewhat mysterious art teacher at Walnut. He preached the value of being observant, since artists must observe to create. He once asked my class who could describe the sculptures at the top of the front entrance to the Walnut building. Most of the class, myself included, did not have a clue. But we soon closely examined the two gargoyle-like faces of the sculptures, and I suspect each of us was just a bit more observant thereafter. Mr. Broz was very worldly, and he loved to talk of subjects other than art. On the last day of school, when signing the *Walnut Cracker* for a student, Mr. Broz found his own picture and drew a small halo around his head, effectively making himself an angel. I watched as he then said to the child, "You will remember this for the rest of your life." Whether this was a daunting prediction or a real curse, I wasn't sure. I don't know about the other kid, but I never forgot it.

Mr. Flanagan (ninth grade): Mr. Flanagan taught me ninth-grade Junior Business. Unlike most, he was not much of a disciplinarian, though he was an excellent teacher. One day Lyle Flebbe walked into the room just as class was about to start. First, Lyle flung open a window, causing a strong wind to blow papers everywhere. Then he literally shouted, in a demanding and accusatory tone, to Mr. Flanagan, "What are we going to do today?" The room was silent with apprehension, but Mr. Flanagan did not overreact. Rather, he simply said, "Now, Lyle, calm down, we are going to learn about checking accounts." His favorite phrase, when he saw people clearly looking at other students' papers, was "partnership grade." "Don't look at other papers!" he'd say. "Do you want a partnership grade, where the grade will be divided in half?" No one ever got a partnership grade, but many looked at their neighbor's work.

Mr. Harms (ninth and twelfth grades): Mr. Harms taught me ninth-grade geometry at Walnut, then later moved to Senior, where he taught me twelfth-grade pre-calculus. In addition to being a scratch golfer, he made the complicated theories of geometry understandable, if you put the time into it. It was in his ninth-grade geometry classroom at Walnut that our class heard about the death of John F. Kennedy over the intercom.

Mr. Heeckt (tenth-grade world history): Mr. Heeckt was maybe my most intellectual teacher at Senior. In his world history class, we read, among other works, *The Iliad* and *The Odyssey*. He would walk around the room, much like a college teacher, and lecture without notes on just about any subject. He wanted you to think in new ways with more insight.

One day he began to discuss religion and the afterlife, generally a subject few teachers would have the courage to discuss. He asked our class if we believed in an afterlife. My sense is that virtually every student did, but Mr. Heeckt said, "Well, I have never known anyone who has been there and back, and I have never seen any evidence that an afterlife exists." A few students were a bit shaken by this, and he then said, "You know, I think with just about every one of you, I could provide you with facts that would break you down." He then looked at me and said, "I am not sure if I could break you down, Mike." I wasn't sure if this meant (1) I was an infidel without beliefs, (2) I was so emotionally strong he couldn't touch me, or (3) I simply didn't much care? I now look back at this as some of the strongest praise I've ever received.

This edition of A Distant Mirror will serve as Part 1 of my "Teach Your Children" recollections. Stay tuned in two months for "Teach Your Children, Part 2," which will include my recollections of additional memorable teachers, including Judy Barth, Lillian Willman, Gale Randall, and the iconic and legendary Elmer Kral.

September 2016

Teach Your Children: My Favorite Teachers, Part 2

In the last alumni newsletter, our Distant Mirror looked back in time with my recollections of some of the wonderful teachers in the GIPS system from 1955 to 1967. A single column was not sufficient, however, to celebrate all the teachers I wanted to recall. At that time, I promised (or threatened, depending on your perspective) to do a Part 2 of my teacher recollections in the next newsletter, to recall some other terrific teachers. So here goes.

Mrs. Judy Barth (tenth-grade English and eleventh-grade *Islander* staff): Mrs. Barth was another of the kindly teachers who supported her students both intellectually and emotionally. She was a very popular teacher who supervised the publication of the *Islander* newspaper. She was beloved and known to the *Islander* staff as "Momma Barth."

I was the sports editor both junior and senior years, which was a delight. To have the weekly deadline was a great exercise in discipline and meeting a commitment. I would write my stories and review the stories written by other staff, edit them, and send them downtown to the printer. Then on Thursday afternoon (I think?), the four editors would go downtown to review and do the final edits on the paper and finalize the layout. Then, on Friday, the *Islander* was issued. To see your words in print was, is, and always will be a total joy.

One incident I will never forget was when classmate Mike Gearhart, another student of Mrs. Barth's, was talking to me, knowing that Mrs. Barth was just behind the door and could hear us. He then said, pretending he didn't know she was there, "Gee, Mike, I don't know why you don't like Mrs. Barth, I think she is great." Mrs. Barth was not fooled, however, and emerged smiling, making clear she did get the joke.

Miss Lillian Willman (twelfth-grade history): Miss Willman was a stern, knowledgeable, and very intellectual teacher who made history come alive. She was the first teacher I knew who each day would recommend reading outside sources, in addition to our textbook, to see different approaches to the same history and get a greater sense of the events we studied. Many of us would go to the library before first period to bone up just a bit.

She graded daily performance by use of a note card for each student. She would go through them in turn, calling on maybe five to ten students each class. She would grade you immediately on the quality of your answer to the question she posed. Since you never knew when your card would be up, you pretty much had to be prepared every day. If she ever dropped or shuffled the cards, panic would ensue, since you didn't know now when you would get called on. I think she even purposefully shuffled them from time to time. Once again, classmate Mike Gearhart comes to mind. His card came up, and she asked him if a particular person had been a United States attorney general. Mike hesitated and then boldly declared,

"Well, this person WAS . . ." clearly leading to an affirmative response. At that point Ms. Willman gave a disapproving glance letting Mike know he was wrong, after which Mike quickly changed direction, saying with great emphasis, ". . . NOT an attorney general." Ms. Willman was neither fooled nor amused by Mike's quick turnabout.

Mr. Gale Randall (eleventh-grade trigonometry): In addition to being the varsity basketball coach, Mr. Randall taught eleventh-grade trigonometry. He was good-natured, bright, and an extraordinary teacher. For those who have taken trigonometry, you will recall that much of the homework entailed long, complicated, and involved proofs and problems, where one could make a mistake at any point that would doom the final result. I was then, and am now, astounded that Mr. Randall, when coming across a mistake, would not simply mark the problem incorrect and call it a day. Rather, he would proceed with the analysis to see if the student made the proper steps after the mistake. He then could give a more representative grade. But it was grueling work. It must have taken him hours every night to correct these papers—all this in addition to high-profile coaching duties as varsity basketball coach.

He was amazingly even tempered. I will never forget his response to my very bright classmate Mike George. At the end of each class, after presenting a new concept, Mr. Randall would then proceed to write the next day's assignment on the blackboard (which was actually a "green" board). As the assignment grew longer, Mike would audibly moan and say "Oh no," then "Oh geez" at each new dagger of an assignment. But Mr. Randall did not respond with a disciplinary power move. Rather, he said something to the effect of "Now Mike, this won't be that much, I think it is very doable." Another less-benign encounter between the two occurred when Mike, at the beginning of a basketball practice, decided to stand on a flimsy card table he had pulled near a basket to jump off and dunk the ball. This went badly awry, however, since as he began his leap, his weight caused his foot to break through the top of the table, ending the dunk attempt, leaving him captive with one leg inside the table, and causing some major cuts on Mike's leg. Both Mike and Mr. Randall were less than pleased with this event.

In twelfth grade, I made the varsity basketball team, as a spunky guard with limited skills. I think my selection for varsity was in part a protective measure, since I was the sports editor of the *Islander*. You don't want to offend the wrong people. But my classmate Bob Peterson and I were clearly the eleventh and twelfth men on a twelve-man squad. We rarely played, which was simply a good utilization of talent. I finished the season with one point. Yup. Uno. A singleton. I was 1-2 at the line in a game at Columbus. I will never forget Mr. Randall's actions when a group of our buddies, including Jim Vohland, put up a sign saying "Let Pete and Muck Play." (Muck was my nickname.) Willing to brook no open rebellion, Mr. Randall himself fired over and made them take down the sign. Even then, I realized he was right.

But my most lasting and endearing thought of Gale Randall, who often had coughing spells, was to see him exit the classroom, do some major audible coughing out there, and then come back in, completely composed and professional. I totally loved the guy.

Mr. Elmer Kral (twelfth-grade English): Mr. Kral was, and is, a legend at GISH. He is truly an "icon." Many of you have your own stories, but I will share a few of mine.

He was a fascinating and complicated fellow, a bit quirky for the times in 1967, and thought of as an odd duck. He was tall, thin, intense, and slightly hunched. He actually ran distances for exercise, as long as a mile, which was revolutionary in 1966. He gave assiduous attention to grammar, composition, rhetoric, and even spelling (that's right, spelling as a senior!). Yet at the same time, more than any teacher at GISH, he treated students like adults. He addressed me "Mr. Monk," no longer "Mike." He expected organization and a work ethic. He was a disciplinarian and a taskmaster.

He was not afraid to rank and judge performance. His was not a class in which every child got a trophy. He actually assigned seating at the desks in his classroom by performance. On the right side of the room facing Mr. Kral was what we students called the "smart row." Each row that proceeded to the left was less "smart," if you will, ending with the "dumb" row on the far left. Even more precise, the students in each row were ranked best to worst, front to back. And if your performance merited a change, he would make it. You could move up or down on the scale, and the result was obvious by glancing about the classroom. Without getting too precise, I will abandon false modesty and admit that I was in the "smart" row.

He focused on good writing, using what was essentially the "Strunk and White" approach. He was known for his obsession with the placement of commas. He advocated the use of the semicolon with a conjunction following it, followed, of course, by the comma. He preached brevity and active voice.

But what made him superior in my view was that he exuded a strong love for literature. He conveyed both the satisfaction of reading great works and the need to study and examine great literature closely, line by line. He made clear that some literature would not be immediately accessible. He taught Shakespeare's *Hamlet* and Milton's *Paradise Lost*, for example, with close attention to important passages, which we studied for lengthy periods. He wanted to show the wonder and joy of finally breaking through great literature and grasping its enormous truths.

But even he was not immune to the witty wiles of the perspicacious GI senior. At the outset of one class, the aforementioned Mike George decided to delay the day's lesson with an ingenious approach. At the beginning of class, he asked Mr. Kral, "Who would you say were the top ten authors of all time?" Mr. Kral immediately took the bait and swam with it: "Well, that is a very interesting question. I would think Shakespeare first, of course, and merely by *Paradise Lost* I think Milton has to be in the top ten. Then, well, there is Tolstoy, and you would have to think about Dante. . . ." For a good fifteen minutes Mr. Kral waxed on, eloquently expressing his views on the best authors in history. I then thought the joke was on Mr. Kral, but I now see the joke was on us, since he got us thinking about that very subject, which is not a bad thing. I will also never forget reading *Hamlet* on a basketball bus trip, which demonstrates his impact.

On April 15, 1967, I was sitting in Mr. Kral's class when a note came asking me to come immediately to the office. I couldn't imagine what trouble I must be in, but I dutifully walked to the office with no small apprehension. But what I found was my mother, beaming with pride and showing me the letter admitting me to Harvard College. I was equally proud that at the end of the year, Mr. Kral told me, "I think you will be able to handle the work you will get next year." Thanks in no small part to Mr. Kral's teaching, I was able to handle my college work just fine. Many of the successes I have had are directly attributable not only to his technical instruction, but also to his ability to engender genuine love for good writing and great literature.

The education my generation got at the Grand Island Public Schools was extraordinary. The number of students who went on to achieve remarkable things bears this out. We were fortunate. When speaking with Mr. Kral decades after he taught me, he referred to the 1960s and 1970s as the "golden age." He noted the students were not only well prepared for high school, but also had the family support and discipline to allow teachers to teach at the highest level.

As a final footnote to education in the heartland, I enclose an item that was sent to me by email. I have no idea if it is genuine or totally fabricated. The sender labeled it as the eighth-grade final exam in a school in Salina, Kansas, in 1895. If legitimate, that school in Kansas was one heck of a school.

Eighth-Grade Final Exam
Salina, Kansas, 1895

Grammar (time: 1 hour)

1. Give nine rules for the use of capital letters.
2. Name the parts of speech and define those that have no modifications.
3. Define verse, stanza, and paragraph.
4. What are the principal parts of a verb? Give principal parts of "lie," "play," and "run."
5. Define case; illustrate each case.
6. What is punctuation? Give rules for principal marks of punctuation.
7–10. Write a composition of about 150 words and show therein that you understand the practical use of the rules of grammar.

Arithmetic (time: 1 hour, 15 minutes)

1. Name and define the Fundamental Rules of Arithmetic.
2. A wagon box is 2 ft. deep, 10 feet long, and 3 ft. wide. How many bushels of wheat will it hold?
3. If a load of wheat weighs 3,942 lbs., what is it worth at 50cts/bushel, deducting 1,050 lbs. for tare?
4. District No. 33 has a valuation of $35,000. What is the necessary levy to carry on a school seven months at $50 per month, and have $104 for incidentals?
5. Find the cost of 6,720 lbs. coal at $6.00 per ton.
6. Find the interest of $512.60 for 8 months and 18 days at 7 percent per annum.
7. What is the cost of 40 boards 12 inches wide and 16 ft. long at $20 per meter?
8. Find bank discount on $300 for 90 days (no grace) at 10 percent.
9. What is the cost of a square farm at $15 per acre, the distance of which is 640 rods?
10. Write a bank check, a promissory note, and a receipt.

U.S. History (time: 45 minutes)

1. Give the epochs into which U.S. history is divided.
2. Give an account of the discovery of America by Columbus.
3. Relate the causes and results of the Revolutionary War.
4. Show the territorial growth of the United States.
5. Tell what you can of the history of Kansas.
6. Describe three of the most prominent battles of the Rebellion.
7. Who were the following: Morse, Whitney, Fulton, Bell, Lincoln, Penn, and Howe?
8. Name events connected with the following dates: 1607, 1620, 1800, 1849, 1865.

Orthography (time: 1 hour)

1. What is meant by the following: alphabet, phonetic, orthography, etymology, syllabication?
2. What are elementary sounds? How are they classified?
3. What are the following, and give examples of each: trigraph, subvocals, diphthong, cognate letters, linguals?
4. Give four substitutes for caret "u."
5. Give two rules for spelling words with final "e." Name two exceptions under each rule.
6. Give two uses of silent letters in spelling. Illustrate each.
7. Define the following prefixes and use in connection with a word: bi, dis, pre, semi, post, non, inter, mono, sup.
8. Mark diacritically and divide into syllables the following, and name the sign that indicates the sound: card, ball, mercy, sir, odd, cell, rise, blood, fare, last.
9. Use the following correctly in sentences: cite, site, sight, fane, fain, feign, vane, vain, vein, raze, raise, rays.
10. Write 10 words frequently mispronounced and indicate pronunciation by use of diacritical marks and by syllabication.

Geography (time: 1 hour)

1. What is climate? Upon what does climate depend?
2. How do you account for the extremes of climate in Kansas?
3. Of what use are rivers? Of what use is the ocean?
4. Describe the mountains of North America.
5. Name and describe the following: Monrovia, Odessa, Denver, Manitoba, Hecla, Yukon, St. Helena, Juan Fernandez, Aspinwall, and Orinoco.
6. Name and locate the principal trade centers of the U.S. Name all the republics of Europe and give the capital of each.
7. Why is the Atlantic Coast colder than the Pacific in the same latitude?
8. Describe the process by which the water of the ocean returns to the sources of rivers.
9. Describe the movements of the earth. Give the inclination of the earth.

November 2016

The Fecundity of the Heartland

Growing up in Nebraska in the 1950s and 1960s, I loved our state. I gave due respect to the western meadowlark and the goldenrod, was very proud of our gorgeous capitol building in Lincoln, and worshipped the Cornhusker football teams. I delighted when my Howard School fifth-grade teacher, Lydia Severson, noted that Nebraskans lived longer than average. And Nebraskans were a steady, reliable, self-reliant, considerate, smart, and loving group of people.

But down deep, I sensed that Nebraska was not a cool place. It was not one of the interesting states like New York or Massachusetts or California. We had no Statue of Liberty, no Yankee Stadium, no Old North Church, no Lexington and Concord, no National Mall, no Disneyland. While we had Chimney Rock, it did not seem to measure up to a Yellowstone, a Yosemite, a Grand Canyon, or a Mount Rushmore.

In Grand Island, we grew up in a thriving community surrounded by gently rolling cornfields and nurtured by the agricultural industry. My friend and 1967 classmate Buzzy Wheeler could speak to the brisk economic climate for those serving this industry. But still, somehow, it was kind of embarrassing. Our vaunted football team was called the Cornhuskers. Rubes husking corn. The rural image did not seem particularly attractive to me. This identity seemed far more lame than the Tigers, the Spartans, the Fighting Irish, the Crimson Tide, or the Cowboys.

When I was about thirteen, I worked a full summer detasseling corn and roguing milo. It was hot, itchy, tiring work, but what a thrill to get that first check, for two weeks of work, for about thirty dollars. I was rich! Still, the cornfields never struck me as having any beauty. Beauty was Niagara Falls. To be called a "farmer" was not a term of praise or respect. My uncle Bud once severely reprimanded me for using the term in a negative way, and I never again used the term derisively.

After high school, I was off to Cambridge, Massachusetts, for college, and then to Philadelphia for law school. Then came marriage and two children. After two years in Brookline, Massachusetts, we moved to the Los Angeles area, where we have lived since 1976. My family and I have had wonderful lives in California. We enjoyed the ridiculously perfect weather and cultural opportunities. We enjoyed the major league sports teams, world-class restaurants, and the beauty of the California coast. We have seen concerts, Super Bowls, World Series games, the 1994 World Cup, NBA Finals games, Rose Bowls, the Rose Parade, and the 1984 Olympics. We are regulars at the latest art house movies, we see terrific opera and theater, and we've seen extraordinary art exhibits, from King Tut to David Hockney. We were blessed with good friends and excellent schools and eventually saw our first two grandchildren born in California in 2010 and 2012.

Throughout this period of forty years on the West Coast, we have always maintained roots in the Midwest, since most of my family remains in Nebraska, and my wife's family has had a cottage on Lake Okoboji in northwestern Iowa since 1961. I first went to the cottage in 1970. We have generally spent a week or more each summer enjoying what is as close to a "resort" as Iowa can claim.

About four years ago my wife and I began to spend nearly seven months of the year at the lake house, where I work remotely from my office on the cottage porch. Friend and 1966 GISH graduate David Rowland lives just a mile down the road. I fly back to California two or three times a summer for business, but I am about half retired. Spending seven months in Iowa has the added advantage of being little more than three hours from Minneapolis, where our daughter and son-in-law and two grandchildren now live.

Over the last five years or so, I have had an increasingly strong sense of well-being and comfort when I return to the Midwest. The once-quiet streets of fashionable coastal Santa Monica have become much more crowded. The freeways more clogged. The general feeling of goodwill I have historically enjoyed in Santa Monica is being ever so slightly reduced by the more aggressive, less considerate behavior I see. I have thrived in the competitive California legal world and have no fear of dealing with adverse circumstances, but things seem less gentle and gracious than they did twenty years ago.

But when I return to the Midwest, the difference is now pronounced. Upon landing in Minneapolis, the courteous people, the more open spaces, and the welcoming Midwestern landscape provide an immediate comfort. There is a more considerate attitude, a more Midwestern tolerance.

A couple of years back, driving from Minneapolis to Lake Okoboji amidst the ripe midsummer corn and soybean fields, I was overcome suddenly by how beautiful, bounteous, and miraculous this farmland really is. The gentle, sloping, green landscape stretched for miles, with a clear view of the horizon on all sides.

Picturesque grain silos and small farms dotted the landscape, well maintained and prosperous in appearance. A gloriously blue sky was liberally scattered with fluffy cumulus clouds and created a gorgeous blue-and-white palette in the sky, as far as the eye could see. What then struck me was the ever-so-obvious, but yet unfathomable enormity of the miracle of our lives. We live on a sphere hurtling through the cosmos, yet are blessed with a climate in which we can live, and an abundance of plants and crops that sustain us. As human beings we have the skills to manage and grow the food we need. The Midwest feeds much of the country, if not world. And this fecundity is simultaneously beautiful. This past August, while visiting my 1967 classmate and buddy Jeff Greenberger in Chicago, at the Art Institute, we saw some Edward Hopper paintings of Midwestern agricultural landscapes that brilliantly portrayed the beauty I now see.

In the spring, on this drive, I see the first barely visible buds of the corn and beans creating a light verdant landscape. In midsummer, the landscape is of mature green corn, and later in the fall, the green leaves are drying, yellowing, and nearly ready for harvest. And now in October, as I write this, most of the corn and soybeans have been harvested, still leaving the brown rolling fields and the broad horizon. I enjoy the same calm, serenity, and incredible abundance.

I will always enjoy Santa Monica, but more and more I experience this strong euphoria just being back in a land where the openness creates for me a freedom, a security, and a comfort. The comparative ease of life in the Midwest always amazes me. Two years ago, I had to register the car I keep in Iowa with Iowa plates. My California DMV experiences involved waits of up to an hour or two, confusing lines for different purposes, and generally harried, humorless people with whom you are dealing. Not so at the DMV office in Spirit Lake, Iowa. When I stepped into the office, there were four women working at desks behind a single counter. I was the only customer. As I walked in, they all looked up and smiled at me.

A very friendly lady came over to help me. All I had was the pink slip for the car. Within fifteen minutes, she had given me my registration and actual plates, not even having seen the car, with no questions about insurance or smog. This was extraordinary.

My local bank in Okoboji, Iowa, is equally amazing. After having an account for a year or two, they now recognize me and will cash my checks without even looking at my ID. Never a traffic jam, never a parking problem, never a line at the post office. And this is 2016. I have slowly realized that I am most happy and content in the rural Midwest.

Maybe part of my newly found appreciation for my agrarian roots stems from the fact that my late father-in-law owned and operated a large farm in Missouri, and when he passed away in 2008, my wife and I took over operation of the farm. I am now the very farmer that I did not appreciate as a child. But I saw my father-in-law's love for the land he farmed. In his failing years, his greatest pleasure was simply to be driven around the farm to see the progress of the crops. Yeah, I know, "The red earth of Tara!"

But I have now realized that my current fondness for the Midwest is not just a rebirth of the positive feelings in my youth, but rather a new, more mature, and far greater appreciation for life in the heartland.

January 2017

The Books of My Youth: Chip Hilton

Some terrific literature for schoolchildren greatly influenced me as a youth in the late 1950s and early 1960s. My generation enjoyed several wonderful series of books, from the Nancy Drew mysteries to the Hardy Boys books to the Henry Huggins series (featuring, of course, Beezus and Ramona), by the dear Beverly Cleary. My personal favorite was the series of Chip Hilton books, by the wonderful author Clair Bee.

Clair Bee was himself a famous athlete and successful college coach at Long Island University in New York. From 1931 to 1951 his basketball teams won 95 percent of their games and had two undefeated seasons. Late in his career, between 1948 and 1966, he wrote twenty-three Chip Hilton books, roughly one book per year. I began to read these books when I was at Howard School in about

1960. They are directed generally at preteens and young teenagers. But later, even as a high schooler, I once again became fascinated with them and reread many of them, with renewed appreciation.

As an adult in my late fifties, I began a quest on eBay to purchase and reread every book in the series, and I did, completing the collection of twenty-three books by forking over $300 or so for the rare final book, *Hungry Hurler*. Bee's family published one more book that Bee had written but not published, *Fiery Fullback*, in 2002.

The mere names of the books make a sports fan's mouth water:

1. *Touchdown Pass* (1948)
2. *Championship Ball* (1948)
3. *Strike Three!* (1949)
4. *Clutch Hitter* (1949)
5. *A Pass and a Prayer* (1951)
6. *Hoop Crazy* (1950)
7. *Pitchers' Duel* (1950)
8. *Dugout Jinx* (1952)
9. *Freshman Quarterback* (1952)
10. *Backboard Fever* (1953)
11. *Fence Busters* (1953)
12. *Ten Seconds to Play!* (1955)
13. *Fourth Down Showdown* (1956)
14. *Tournament Crisis* (1957)
15. *Hardcourt Upset* (1957)
16. *Pay-Off Pitch* (1958)
17. *No-Hitter* (1959)
18. *Triple-Threat Trouble* (1960)
19. *Backcourt Ace* (1961)
20. *Buzzer Basket* (1962)
21. *Comeback Cagers* (1963)

22. *Home Run Feud* (1964)
23. *Hungry Hurler* (1966)
24. *Fiery Fullback* (2002)

Set in an unnamed state resembling Pennsylvania, Ohio, Indiana, or some such middle America location, the books tell the story of Chip Hilton, a nearly perfect high school and college athlete and human being, a personification of what we all should be. Chip was the only son of Mary Hilton and his father, the elder "Chip" Hilton, himself a storied athlete at Valley Falls High and, later, State University. The elder Chip died in a pottery accident while saving the life of a fellow worker. Chip's mother then carried on and supported her beloved son, Chip.

The books generally follow Chip through each sports season, one book for each sport, each year, starting with football season in his junior year in high school. They proceed to cover every football, basketball, and baseball season through his junior and senior years at Valley Falls High School and through his four years at State University.

Chip is a gifted athlete in all sports. He combines wonderful physical skills with a dedication to practice, technique, determination, and team concepts. He usually leads his team to the state championship, while simultaneously being the center of a wonderful group of friends, working part-time at the local drugstore to help his mother with the bills, and much like the Hardy Boys, solving mysteries along the way. He often faces the adversity of a teammate or small group of teammates who resent Chip and his friends. But by the end of the book, Chip has made these adversaries his friends and loyal supporters. Chip also finds time to help solve and resolve problems of his friends and, occasionally, to foil the nefarious criminal pursuits of adults.

Chip's loyal group of friends include Speed Morris, Red Schwartz, Biggie Cohen, and Soapy Smith. Two Jewish names and a Smith and a Morris. Last summer, when reading about the Alaskan gold rush, I discovered that the most notorious criminal in Skagway, Alaska, was a man named "Soapy" Smith. Another example of Clair Bee's forward-looking perspective occurs in *Hoop Crazy*, in which Chip loyally supports the progress of an African American teammate on the Valley Falls basketball team.

To me, the Chip Hilton books represent a page in our American history, as they depict the values of the 1940s and 1950s. The values Chip most notably displays are loyalty, honesty, sportsmanship, friendship, taciturnity, self-reliance, and modesty. For Chip, the worst trait possible is to be a tattletale. He never rats out the bad guy, even if his forbearance is to his own detriment. Equally important is self-reliance. If you get into a tough situation, handle it yourself. Do not blame others for the results of your own actions.

I do not suggest the values the Chip Hilton books espouse are always better than the current values or that since the good old days everything has gone to Hades. Not so. In fact, some of the values in the Chip Hilton books would now be seen as improper and uncivilized. So, while sometimes better and sometimes worse, they are different values. For example, the strong tendency for Chip and his friends to try to solve problems on their own might today seem unwise where the matter should be handled by authorities. Indeed, Chip at times reluctantly engages in fistfights when forced to do so, certainly not the current approach to resolving problems. But his motives are pristine.

In the opening book, *Touchdown Pass*, Chip not only leads Valley Falls to the state football championship, but also overcomes a group of three teammates who resent Chip and his friends. In the beginning, the enemies flaunt Coach Rockwell's orders to try to embarrass Chip, but Chip never tells the coach, instead taking the blame. Chip's complete unwillingness to tell the coach that these troublemakers are the ones who refused to run the play the coach ordered is at one level noble. At another level, it shows an approach bereft of the simple communication skills that help a team. But it does show his enemies his integrity, and by the end of the book, of course, the former enemies realize Chip's character and become loyal supporters.

In the same book, Chip also helps the father of his friend Taps Browning, who was fired from his job as chemist at the local pottery. Mr. Browning was wrongfully blamed for bad mixes of clay that produced damaged products. Chip, in addition to working, playing sports, studying, and tending to his mother, takes turns with Biggie Cohen and Speed Morris spending entire nights at the pottery on watch until they catch the disgruntled employee who tainted the clay. Chip then succeeds in getting his friend's father's job back

One of the opening scenes in *Touchdown Pass* reflects the different culture of the times. A jealous football teammate purposely hits Chip late several times and injures him in a practice. But Chip does not complain to the coach, does not retaliate, does not tell his mother to intervene, and does not get a lawyer to sue the miscreant. Rather, he sucks it up, perseveres, and eventually the perpetrator is kicked off the team. Despite this incident and a history of this person plaguing Chip, when the antagonist later is threatened by gamblers to whom he owes money, Chip and his friends come to his rescue.

Chip not only has a job throughout high school, but he also works throughout college. He works in the back room ordering supplies at the popular local hangout, a drugstore with a lunch counter, booths, and a soda jerk making ice-cream sundaes. Chip spends every waking hour either playing sports, doing homework, working at the drugstore, or spending time with his mother and friends. Even in college, Chip has a term-time job, studies late into the night, constantly writes letters home to his mother, and practices and plays sports. He steadfastly refuses to live in the sports dormitories or accept a scholarship, thinking it would give him special privileges that would be unfair.

Another wonderful aspect of these books, and of the 1940s and 1950s in general, is that high school sports were extremely prominent, sort of the only show in town. The local press covers each game as if it were the Super Bowl. The stands are packed with everyone in town. The local radio station covers every game. It is the talk of the town, from the soda fountain to the factories. After a big win, the fans pour onto the field and do a "snake dance" parading around the field in a conga line of sorts as they celebrate.

But these were the days when television might broadcast one baseball, football, or basketball game a week. Indeed, I do not recall a single reference to television in the entire series of Chip Hilton books. There were no ESPN channels, no smartphones, no StubHub, and no dizzying series of twelve college basketball games and four NBA games on television every day.

In the Chip Hilton books, the newspaper is the primary source of news and a staple of the community. The local sports writers play a large role. I now feel like a relic in this regard in 2017. I have three newspapers delivered to my door each morning. I love the tactile pleasure of holding and reading the printed word on paper while I have my coffee, half grapefruit, and Grape-Nuts. But I know the local newspaper is a dying animal, and one wonders how long many will exist. Most Americans under forty, I suspect, do not subscribe to a single newspaper but get all their news online or on television. Granted, we now all know within ten minutes if Tom Brady or David Ortiz, not to mention Justin Bieber or Taylor Swift, do anything exciting, since it is tweeted, posted, blogged, and blasted through cyberspace in a heartbeat.

The structure of each Chip Hilton book is nearly identical. Chip is the very quiet and modest leader of a great group of friends. His teams have problems early in the season, both with the right strategy for the team to win and with jealous teammates who undercut team morale. Yet Chip wins over the enemies, who in the next book are his loyal friends. He finds some local civic or community wrong to right and proceeds to solve the problem or bring the criminal to justice. The team eventually jells, and aided by Chip's extraordinary play and the loyalty of his teammates, they virtually always win the state championship. Clair Bee also sprinkles in lots of wisdom regarding sports techniques, different offenses and defenses, and training. It is like eating candy.

This structure ironically reminds me of many of the novels of Charles Dickens. The protagonist is beset by challenges and difficulties, and dastardly cruel villains plague his every step. Yet in the end, good wins out over evil. David Copperfield triumphs over Uriah Heep and is able to help his friends Mr. Wickfield and Mr. Micawber.

The Chip Hilton books exude an aura of community, friendship, integrity, and the love of sports. There are challenges to overcome, but there is great joy when the difficulties are surmounted. The books are poignant and heartwarming as well. Only two hundred pages or so, they are a very quick read. I would recommend anyone try one and take yourself back into a very different time in America, a time of more innocence than we now enjoy. If you doubt me, talk to GISH 1970 graduate Dan Greenberger, who once considered writing a modern story using the Chip Hilton structure and values. I would love it.

March 2017

May 1, 1957: The May Day Dance on the Green

Doris Dubbs, more commonly known to everyone she knew as "Gramma," got out of the 1954 Buick with the three decorative holes on each side of the car, glancing at Howard Elementary School with both assurance and uncertainty. She was a spunky lady, and at the age of forty-seven, she was already the mother of four and the grandmother of three. The prospect of going to see her eldest grandchild, Mike Monk, perform at the annual May Day "Dance on the Green," filled her with both pride and anticipation. The Dubbs family had moved to Grand Island only three years before, and she was still making friends with the parents of Mike's classmates. Though a young grandmother, Doris was prematurely wrinkled due to a major rapid weight loss she experienced in her early forties. No one seemed to even consider her age, though, since her swaggering confidence and good humor assaulted everyone she met.

Howard School was about seven blocks from Mike's home at 317 East 12th Street. It was just two blocks down to 10th Street, where Mike's friend George Ayoub lived. One then proceeded about five blocks west, to 10th and Cedar, to reach the modern brick grade school. Doris's drive was, of course, a simple one with few other cars on the streets. In this sleepy town of twenty-five thousand or so, the pace was measured and comfortable, even in your Buick cruising the streets. Children under age five, too young for kindergarten, played casually in their yards, or rode through the neighborhood on their tricycles with little restriction. The concept of nursery school or preschool was generally foreign to the mothers in town. Preschool-age children for the most part entertained and amused themselves, alternately playing with the neighborhood kids, pressing their mothers for "something to do," or inventing endless games, projects, plots, and dramas to fill their lives of leisure.

Doris walked along the cement sidewalk ringing Howard School and headed toward the grassy pasture between the two wings of the school. As she approached, she saw a gaily colored Maypole had been erected in the center of the green grass. Folding chairs had been placed in two rows encircling the field in which the dances were to occur. Doris was never one to hesitate, and she characteristically walked directly to the seats she thought presented the best view. She saw a single empty seat in the second row and sat down quickly, involuntarily smiling a big smile and saying hello to the woman seated to her left.

Ellen Parmley, the woman to Doris's left, returned her smile and extended her hand to Doris. As Doris shook the lady's hand, she saw a woman younger than herself, likely in her thirties, with a radiant smile on a face that was badly scarred by a burn or birthmark of some kind. Doris first experienced a brief feeling of pain and sympathy for the woman, thinking "that poor dear, to have gone through something like that." Within minutes, however, Doris had lost consciousness that a scar even existed, engrossed entirely in the lively personality of the mother of Bob, Mike, Cindy, and Dave Parmley.

"Well hello," repeated Doris, "I'm Doris Dubbs, and I'm here to see my grandson Mike, who is dancing with the second grade. He's that little blond guy over there who needs to pull his pants up a little."

"Why hello," said Ellen, "I'm Ellen Parmley, and I believe my little guy Mike in the second grade is a friend of your Mike. You see, we just moved to Grand Island this year from Mead, Nebraska. I can't believe it has taken this long to meet you, as much as Mike and Mike have been playing together."

"Oh, your little Mike is a cutie," said Doris. "He's a little stinker sometimes too."

"He sure is, Doris," said Ellen, "and you know I have Bob in the third grade, Cindy who's just turned five, and then little Davie."

"How old is Davie now?" asked Doris.

"He's not even two yet—and he may be my cutest little guy yet—but I sometimes wonder if he isn't going to be my biggest headache."

"Well, if it isn't one thing it's twenty-one with a young one that age. I'll bet you a dollar to a donut that they are all the best headaches you'll ever have."

"But tell me," said Ellen, "how many grandchildren do you have?"

"Well, I'll tell you—right now I've got my three daughters and my three grandchildren all living under my roof, which gives me plenty of help when I need it!"

"My goodness gracious, Doris, I didn't realize you all lived together. Now Ramona is Mike's mother, right?"

"That's right," said Doris. "And Ramona also has Mike's little sister, Patty, who just turned five like your little Cindy. Ramona is the sweetest girl in town, but she's had a couple of tough-luck marriages that just haven't worked out. She divorced Mike's father when Mike was not quite two years old, I think mostly because she was too young to be married. She was married at age sixteen and gave birth to Mike two months before she was eighteen. Then she married Patty's father, a nice guy who just couldn't get his drinking under control, and she had to get out of that one."

"And your other two daughters?" asked Ellen.

"Jerenne is Ramona's younger sister, and she and her boy, Randy, also live with us. Then there's my youngest girl, Cindy, or Lucinda Sue, who is four, a year younger than Patty and Randy, who are five, like your Cindy," explained Doris. "Ramona and Jerenne are both working, but they are not ready just yet to get out on their own. And I'll tell you, those little ones can keep you running, but they get in line a lot faster for ol' Gramma than they do for their mothers."

By this time, the dances had begun, and Doris and Ellen were watching the sixth graders square-dance. Since neither Mike was involved yet, the ladies continued their conversation in a more confidential manner.

"Well, Doris, you sound like you have your hands full. I know how Grammas can become a real convenient babysitter."

"You're right about that, but you know how darn cute those kids can be, just when you want to smack them."

"Oh, I know," said Ellen. "My Mikey is just a cute little feller, but he brings me a couple of headaches too. Mrs. Moore sent him down to the kindergarten class, along with Steve Schroeder, for acting up; and you know, I don't know if Mike even minded. He came home from school and was a little embarrassed, but he said the nap was fun. That little guy—I just have to laugh."

"Oh, I know, I came home last summer and Randy, Patty, and Cindy had played 'barbershop.' They got out my good pinking shears, my best scissors, and started cutting each other's hair. They couldn't do much but hack at Randy's. But the girls both had long, beautiful pigtails, and they had cut off both of Cindy's pigtails and one of Patty's when I walked in on them. 'Jesus Christ!' I said—you've got to excuse my language, but I was an angry grandmother! I didn't know whether to cut off the other pigtail or not."

By this time, the second grade had assembled for the French folk dance they were to present. Mike had told his Gramma how his teacher, Mrs. Martin, said it was very important as the dancers circled at the end of the dance for the children to kick their knees very high. She emphasized the need for "each and every" child to kick high together to achieve the desired result.

Ellen, too, had heard of the practice time given to the folk dance and she watched closely, spotting her son Mike. Doris quickly found her grandson Mike in the circle of second graders and also recognized Steve Schroeder between Mike Parmley and her Mike Monk. As the dancers began, Mike Monk caught his Gramma's eye and flashed a quick smile, but he was careful not to miss a step and returned his concentration to the steps they had practiced.

Like many of the second-grade boys, Mike Parmley wore a nice white shirt with a black bow tie the color of his thick, dark-rimmed glasses. He liked square dancing but tried to avoid the girl with the sweaty hands, a type that bothered Parm more than most. But any activity that involved jumping and running was fine with him. As Parm rounded the circle near his mother, he also caught his mother's eye and they exchanged broad grins and mutual enjoyment of the festivities. Parm felt good when his mother was near him, and to bring her to laughter gave him as much pure pleasure as anything. Today he was performing for Ellen, and he tried his best to perform the dance perfectly.

Steve Schroeder was bored with the whole dancing business. Girls were the last things he wanted to be near, not to mention touch. He also felt stupid dancing dumb foreign dances that no one danced in real life. He thought it was particularly humiliating to have to do all this in front of all the kids in the whole school, mothers dressed up in dresses and hats, and all the teachers and the principal, just waiting for you to make a mistake. Schro mechanically went through the steps, clearly the least enthusiastic dancer in the second grade. As the dance built to the climax, the children, about thirteen girls and thirteen boys, began to prance in a circle. This was the part of the dance where the knees were to be lifted high. Mike Parmley and Mike Monk both kicked as high as they could, prancing like show horses. By this time Schro was totally humiliated in his own mind. He avoided his mother's eyes and trotted along slowly, failing completely to raise his knees, shuffling along with a frown on his face.

Mike Monk saw Schro shuffling ahead of him and whispered loudly, "Schro, kick your knees, you dummy!" He frowned at his good friend.

Schro looked back at Mike, slowed his pace even more, and for the first time all day, felt good. He broke into a huge grin while looking at Mike. Suddenly, Mike thought Schro shuffling along was the funniest thing in the world. Both boys were soon laughing loudly as they completed the final steps in the dance. Parm saw Schro, too, and grinned without knowing exactly what was so funny.

"Would you look at that Steve Schroeder," said Doris. "'I don't what he's trying to do. You know, I think that boy Steve isn't going to take much baloney when he grows up."

"It was a real nice dance no matter what," said Ellen. "My family is from Greece, and I love seeing the different dances from other countries. I think it's so good for the kids to get a chance to see something from a different land."

The concluding performance of the "Dance on the Green" spring celebration was the Maypole Dance, where the fifth graders danced in a circle, each holding a very long ribbon extending down from the top of the Maypole. As the dance proceeded, the children danced in and out among each other, slowly weaving the ribbons into a tight braid coming down the Maypole. As more and more of each dancer's ribbon became woven down the pole, each dancer necessarily drew closer to the center, and the radius of the circle methodically shortened. As Doris watched the event, the individual dancers seemed to fade from view, becoming part of an organic whole. The colored ribbons seemed almost to move of themselves, like a machine systematically producing a precise, beautiful, and inevitable pattern that no one could change.

May 2017

Victoria's Tent Rules at Age Six

This past Friday, March 10, 2017, my daughter posted on Facebook that my six-year-old, first-grade granddaughter, Victoria, had built a "tent" by draping blankets over the couch and some chairs, held in place by pillows. But more importantly, she had drafted, numbered, and written out, all by herself, a set of tent rules, which were taped to the side of the tent. The "Tent Ruls" are set forth below, verbatim and with her original spelling:

Tent Ruls

1. The entr for the tent is were you entr the door
2. Be Saf
3. Have Fun

4. No Pushing
5. No skraching
6. No Biding
7. If you have to go to the bathroom get owt qwic and go.
8. And do not take off the pilows.
9. Be carfle with the chars.
10. Mak friends.
11. Be nice.
12. No fiting

Thak You

I was initially amused by the fact that she would even write down the rules. I am continually impressed that she feels comfortable writing long notes, letters, cards, and lists without agonizing over the precise spelling. This is the approach in the Minneapolis public school she attends, and it is, in my view, very wise. The spelling gets better all the time, but she feels very comfortable composing. And the phonetic spelling she uses shows, in some cases, how the word maybe should be spelled.

Upon reflection, however, it appeared to me that this list was much more than just a set of tent rules. The list seems rather to be a very succinct and wise list on how to live one's life generally. Yes, "Rules for Life." Should we not all seek to follow the rules of "Be saf, have fun, no pushing, no skraching, no biding, mak friends, be nice, and no fiting?" If more adults were to follow these simple rules, we would all be much better off.

Also, it is of course good to know that the "entr for the tent is were you entr the door." You have to know where to get in, for goodness' sake. And maybe the best rule of all for life is "when you have to go to the bathroom get owt qwic and go." In my own life, I would have avoided much agony had I followed that rule. Equally important is to "not take off the pilows" (the structural foundation of the tent). Finally, we all should not only be "carfle with the chars" but "carfle" in all aspects of our life.

I promise to keep you posted if further rules are adopted.

July 2017

Ode to the High School Class of 1967

(50th Reunion in 2017)

I.

This modest bit of poetry
Is all about our Class, you see.

The names bring floods of memories
Of loves, of friends, of shapely knees.

The female names are maiden ones,
No married names will you hear sung,

As if we were in school again,
Less taxing for the aging brain.

But now with little more ado,
Class of '67, a salute to you!

II.

Stanley Browning, Susan Kane,
Jan Kirkpatrick, Linda Lane,

Peggy Holden, Carmen Bahr,
Carletta Leibhart, Michael Carr.

Mary Jo Frey, Sharolyn Molle,
Randy Olson, Hervey Cole,

Cheryl Harrison, Sandy Merhring,
Stylish whatever they were wearing.

Rita Brabender, Christie Shell,
Lou Ann Brittain, Sandy Spell.

Luebke, Farlee, Flebbe, and Wilke,
Lykke, Linke, Furby, and Zuelke,

Dennis Glover, Timothy Spiehs,
Euguene Crist, and Lana Weise.

Jimmy Vohland, Terry Virus,
Mickey Mantle, Roger Maris.

Jim Johansen, Terry Trentman,
Michael Gearhart, Gloria Fenton.

Pamela Cramer, Sherry Schultz,
Douglas Crouch, Patricia Pelz.

Dixie Davis, Mercy me!
And lovely Kathy Gregory.

David Weeks and Dennis Stark,
Janie Plautz and Robert Clark.

Hickstein, Meedel, Woody, and Greenie,
Danny Chrystal, and Isotope Feeney.

Jimmy Hines and Debbie Grimes,
Recall the distant high school times.

Patty Hartley, Samie Rank,
Elmer Kral, and Barbara Banks.

The classy Boyds, Debbie and Suze,
You remember Betty Kruse.

And Ron Kruse, too, after all these years,
I remember him playing "96 Tears"!

Eulalia Hoback, Elaine Hodtwalker,
Jackie Learned, Muriel Stalker,

Migrants to California's farm,
Stormy, Bobine, Mucker, and Parm.

Roz Ritchie, too, chose a West Coast life,
A Wellesley classmate of my wife.

Roy Rogers and Mike "Dougger" George,
Dee Ann Crist, and Billy Barge.

Donna Anderson, Carroll Brown,
Valera Richards went to town!

Darrell and David, they were the Hills,
Floyd McMullen, and Connie Mills.

Hail to the Rosses, Tricia and Ken,
They brought us together, now women and men.

And Trish, lest anyone not see,
You may have known as Pat Embree,

Clayton, Mark and Clayton, Steve,
Both had plenty up their sleeve.

Susan Helie and Richard Reed
Few of us, then, smoked much weed.

Our friends, the Schuylers, Barb and Jerry,
Then the Houses, Jim and Terry.

Warren Lautenschlager and Bennie Stump,
Dave Glass was better known as "Hump."

Eric "Cocker" and Joel "Specker,"
Galen Loomis and Peggy Decker.

The Schroeders, Jiminie and John,
Joanie Marland, next Paul Hahn,

Huwalt, Ewolt, Lanman, and Larson,
Linda During and William Carson.

Peggy Burger, William Sartin,
Lucy Manette, and Sydney Carton.

Nancy Engle and Terri White,
Van the Man Coker, Edgar Wright.

The Bakers were two, Nick and Glenn,
Loretta Wilson, and Arnold Wenn.

Peterson, Patterson, Van Pelt, and Van Horn,
Jackson, Hahn, and of course Rip Torn.

The Woitaszewskis, Ron and Don,
They raised pigeons on their lawn.

Bill Dombrowski, Don Opocensky,
Can't forget Jerome Urbanski,

Mark and Marilyn, the siblings Stelk,
Yolanda Inguanzo and Lawrence Welk,

Rickie Drawbaugh, Charlene Benson,
Tom Henry, too, but not Jim Henson.

Terry Dellegge, Ronald Gaddy,
Debby Gaskill, Wanda Eddy.

Vidette Gustin, Susan Kroll,
I'd gladly take them for a stroll!

Carol Pierce and Mike O'Neil
Made their marks with glee and zeal.

Lockers, notebooks, tests, and alarms,
Coach Bobby Hansen and Roger Harms.

Celestine Mathews, Larry Kelly,
Robert Rutar, and Patty Farlee.

Julie Fishler, Julie Dunham,
Rodney Swanson, Damon Runyan.

The halls in which Dave Townsend went,
Student Council Vice President.

Nelson, Neilson, and Lute did strut,
Craig Scherzberg was a vaulting nut.

The Smiths: Cheryl, Dennis, Pam, Susan, and Tim,
Steve Gardner, too, and Sandra Kehm.

Dean Vavak was an artist true,
AKA Stanley to me and you.

Skiller, Spiehser, and my friend Lamp,
Ellen Pilmer and Terrance Stamp.

Nancy Samway, Charlie Ruhl,
Good folks who were never cruel.

Jim Mitchell of course and Janet Pace,
Gretchen Vieregg's charm and grace.

Katie Hauschild, Stanley French,
Carol Mader, Jimmie Munch.

Melinda Brockelsky, Lana Hann,
Marilyn Glover, and Zachary, Don.

Nancy Tyson and Marilyn Fore,
Bring back the days of high school yore,

Russell Hiatt, Sandy Steele,
Barbara Graupner, William Thiel.

Howard's dear Gloria Callihan,
Walt Meyer, too, a vaulting man,

Betty Evans and David Wold
Wore Islander colors, purple and gold.

Wayne Moomey, Kaila Leisinger,
Bill Ruben, Diana Kessinger

Keep Donna Dahlke in the loop,
And Judy Kemp, she married Coop!

And Cheryl Ramsey wed Vaughn Truman,
Who could blame her, she's only human.

Don Preisendorf and Sharon Ford,
Vemelle Niemoth is on board.

Cam Edwards singing "Something Stupid,"
He and Diana, touched by Cupid.

Sheila Myers, Sheila Tillman,
Banking mogul Suzanne Oldham.

Carol Carmody, Janet James say hi!
Marylin Oldaker and Elaine Spry,

Steven Taylor, Steven Snyder,
Jeannie Stockman, Jackie Schwieger.

Jim Johanson, Judy Knight,
Chuck Hoffman wed the "Reher" est sight.

Anderson, Gibson, and Paulette Stenka,
Steve Fuller, too, and Willy Wonka.

Kaila's man is Freddie Roeser,
Karen Boltz was no mere poser.

Dave Fuller and Karen Fiedler say hi.
Georgia Sorensen, my oh my!

Pam Schaffitzel and Marlyn Koch,
Chris Benson took it up a notch.

Wrenn Lesher, too, and Darrell Miller,
The clothes we wore were total killer.

Rod Koelling, Sharon Merithew,
Were Islanders, yea, through and through.

Renter's first name, it was Dehn,
Puzzling now and puzzling then.

Dorothy Dehning, she makes them swoon,
Jeanene Kelly and Joe Calhoun.

Diane Schuppan, she's here, too,
A lovely Islander through and through.

Annette Owings, Donna Jordan,
Batman and Commissioner Gordon.

June Hessell and Becky Arnold we knew,
Howard's Billy Murphy is our friend, too.

Linda Mason, Janet James,
Our class was full of charming dames.

A vivid time, so long ago,
Who knew we, now, would view it so?

III.

But now to leave the mirth behind,
Close friends we've lost will flash to mind.

Dave Rombach was our President,
For Secretary, Sue Ann was sent,

I see Sue Ann as Peter Pan, flying on the wire so high,
And Rombach clutching to his feather, running round the track would fly,

And others have left us far too soon,
No chance to see life's evening moon:

They lived, they breathed, we saw them soar,
They passed this way, but are no more.

But all their spirits we embrace,
May they be blessed with loving grace.

September 2017

The Glorious First Day of School

Our Distant Mirror today begins by revisiting the last day of school in fifth grade at Howard School in May 1960. I remember this as a great day. I have a vivid recollection of riding my bicycle home with some friends, thinking that this was as good as it gets. No school for three months, but just an unending string of wonderful lazy days. Pickup baseball games at Howard, going to Pier Park and the "big pool," as we called it, to swim for hours, Monopoly games with the neighbors, going to the summer shows hosted by Wally Kemp at the Grand Theatre, building forts, sleeping in, and trips to the Carnegie Library to get books about sports. I was in heaven. Later that summer, inspired by the Rome Olympics, we had a Neighborhood Olympics, with running races, bike races around the block, high jump, pole vault, broad jump, shot put, and relay races. My summers were fantastic, though I never attended a single day of camp or any real organized activity, except for Little League Baseball.

But as the summer wore on, and the first day of school approached, I remember no sadness or angst at having to return to school, but indeed the opposite. It was incredibly exciting to get back to school. Which teacher would I get for sixth grade? Would I be in the same room as my buddies? What excitement to see the new textbooks and the new classroom. And the first day was of course preceded by getting new school clothes and school supplies.

There is a treasured family photo of me and my mother on the first day of kindergarten in 1954. I had on brand-new blue jeans, bought to last for some time, with the cuffs rolled up about eight inches. A simple white T-shirt and leather shoes completed my attire. My sister Pat and cousin Randy are in the background riding their tricycles, wearing little more than their underwear. The smell of new denim is, to this day, a strong reminder of the first day of school.

Later at Walnut Junior and at Senior High, the joy and excitement of the first day of school was different, but still pronounced. School clothes were a bit more sophisticated then, but still an important ritual, and it was essential to get some of the latest fashions, including one year in high school when one of the cool new madras shirts or belts was essential.

The supplies we purchased were a three-ring notebook with a blue canvas cover, a plastic three-hole pencil case, dividers to separate the materials from each class, and new book covers. The glossy book covers were works of art, with symbols of the Walnut Wildcats or the Senior High Islanders on durable, high-quality paper. We all tended assiduously to the task of putting the book covers on our schoolbooks, taping them on firmly, and proudly viewing the beautiful result.

My first-day-of-school memories are triggered today by my granddaughter Victoria, since I am writing this in early September

2017, on what is her first day of second grade at the Groveland Elementary School in Minnetonka, Minnesota. Things are a bit more organized these days. There was an open house last week, where the second graders, parents, grandparents, and siblings got to see the classroom, see the very desk where Victoria will sit, meet the teacher, and see how well prepared they are for class. A few years back, my sister Pat and I visited Howard just before the first day of school, and I saw impressive organization, with desks, pictures, books, and all aspects of the classroom neat and tidy and ready for the onslaught of enthusiastic youth.

I have learned, however, that the modern student, even in grammar school, needs far more than two No. 2 pencils and a notebook. Indeed, the list that some schools send out is jaw-droppingly long and specific. One list included "300 Ticonderoga pencils, five reams of printer paper, three packs of Post-it notes, two boxes of Kleenex, one potted plant," and on and on. Some schools will have the full packet available for purchase, albeit at an inflated price. But there are also stories of children who are not pleased at getting the government-issue packet but are desperate to pick out the backpack of their choice, with just the colors and design they want.

By the way, no one had a backpack, or even a book bag, in the 1950s or 1960s. We just lugged around our notebook and two or three books for homework in our bare hands, as I recall it. Today, the skinny second graders lug around backpacks seemingly more than half their size.

But the thrill of the new year, the excitement of meeting your classmates, and the desire (for many, but not all) to impress the new teacher still provide great excitement. I remember this pleasing excitement even in college. The way I would shop for classes, in part, was to go to the college bookstore, which had all the books for each class available for purchase. To examine the books, touch their virgin bindings, and decide upon the courses I wanted was for me a real joy. This delicious smorgasbord of academic opportunities and knowledge was all there for the taking. Indeed, even after decades of being out of school, to me the year really begins not in January, but in August or September when school begins.

So as Grand Island students now settle in during the first few weeks of school, I want to say I envy you. Don't view this ritual as a dreary obligation, but as an exciting time that many of you will remember for the rest of your life. I hope you all get the teacher you want, the classmates you want, and the best located locker. You deserve no less.

November 2017

James's "Golden Birthday" in Italy, July 10, 1989

The Monks' rented car cruised along the Italian Autostrada north toward Lake Como, and James Monk for about the one hundredth time that afternoon realized with delight that this was his "golden birthday" and that he was now ten years old on the tenth of July.

"Ten on the tenth," thought James, as he twisted and adjusted the arms, legs, and head of Michelangelo, the rubber action figure from the television show *Teenage Mutant Ninja Turtles*. James's dad, Mike, and sister, Susannah, had purchased Michelangelo at a toy shop near the Piazza di Spagna in Rome three days earlier. Along with Michelangelo, James had been given various other birthday toys designed principally to satisfy a boy's natural desire to get a fair share of pure toys and a minimum of sweaters and socks. This desire was of course particularly strong on a golden birthday.

James had become familiar with the concept of a golden birthday at age nine in the summer of 1988 at his grandparents' lake house in Okoboji, Iowa. James, his mother, Janet, and sister, Susie, usually spent three or four weeks there each summer, with Mike joining them for a week or so. They slept late, swam, watched television game shows, read, and goofed around. Olivia Watson from next door at the lake had explained that a golden birthday was when you were as old as the number of the day on which you were born.

"You know, like you are five on the fifth or for you, Susie, twenty-five on the twenty-fifth," explained Olivia. Susie, who was then thirteen, had been born on May 25, 1976.

"So my golden birthday is next year, when I am ten on the tenth," said James.

James's father, Mike, was the first to glimpse Lake Como as the car went down the winding road through the mountains near the lake. "Well, now I'm not one to go out on a limb, but I bet five thousand lire that this is Lake Como, gang!"

"Wow, that's cool," said Susie.

They were all taken by the beauty of the view from the steeply sloping mountains that closely framed the narrow southern end of the lake. They were headed to the Villa d'Este in Cernobbio, a fancy Italian hotel right on the lake.

"James," said Janet, "do you realize we are staying at probably our nicest hotel on the whole trip here in Lake Como, and it happens to be on your birthday?"

"I know, Mom, three swimming pools, one indoors. I wish they had motorcycles to rent too."

"I'm looking forward to the restaurant," Janet admitted. "Your father and I had a great dinner there the last time we were in Italy."

"As long as they have spaghetti Bolognese, I'll be fine," said James, who had seen his fondness for this basic Italian dish grow to where he had two servings at one sitting at the Buca dell'Orafo in Florence.

"Oh, I'm so sick of your spaghetti Bolognese, James, I could scream," said Susie.

They wound down the road, exited the Autostrada, paid the toll, and drove more slowly through the little villages ringing the lake. The signs to Villa d'Este were as prominently displayed as the arrows to the various villages, and the Monks' car soon entered the spacious grounds of the hotel. After they checked in, they secured their two adjoining rooms. Janet and Mike wanted to unpack a bit before donning their swimsuits. The only quirk they encountered was the porter's confusion as to what to do with the Trojan War helmet and toy sword James had received in Athens for an early birthday present. Mike assured the porter that they wanted the helmet and sword in the room and not left in the car, knowing James would not want to be far from such important possessions.

James and Susie then headed toward the pools on their own, semi-experienced travelers as they were. Janet and Mike soon joined the kids and stationed themselves on the deck of a pool that actually floated on the lake. Susie and James then decided to explore the indoor pool. Janet swam laps at the floating pool, while Mike dozed and read as the spirit moved him.

After about half an hour, Mike joined the kids in the indoor pool, partly to see if they were alive, and partly to check out the pool for himself.

"Dad, this place is great! I love this hotel," said James. "Come swim with me. They have this huge water jet underneath the water that you swim against, and it is so strong that it propels you back!"

"And Dad," said Susie, "they have two roped-off lanes just for laps, and the water is extremely warm. It's like a bath."

Mike did a few "can openers" into the pool and let James and Susie dive from his shoulders. He then swam a couple of laps, returned to the floating pool, and went back to his dozing and reading, with Janet reading beside him.

About an hour later Susie sprinted onto the deck of the floating pool. She spied her mom and dad and announced, "James and I met two children from Ireland, and we've been playing with them. How long are we going to be swimming, since they've asked James and me to have a drink with them at the bar after swimming. The girl is about my age and the boy is one year older. They like playing with James too."

"What are you guys going to have at the bar, a vodka tonic?" asked Mike.

"No, Dad," Susie said, brushing her father off, "we'll have Coke or Coke Light or Evian or something. Can we?"

"Sure," said Mike. "We'll go change soon so you can make your date. We have dinner reservations at eight, you know."

"I know, Dad, but we have three hours," said Susie.

Just then James sprinted onto the deck and addressed his parents breathlessly. "I've got to go change, I'm having a drink at the bar with our new friends, let's go!"

"Okay . . . relax," his father pleaded as they proceeded up to the rooms.

After the children went down for their drink with their new friends, Janet and Mike enjoyed a moment of quiet and reading by themselves. Mike went out to read on the balcony outside their room, positioned himself on the chair with his legs up on the little patio table, and began to read *I, Claudius*. The balcony presented a gorgeous view of Lake Como and the opposite shore, which rose precipitously and was a misty dark green in color. Various houses, buildings, and what seemed like villas, or modest castles, dotted the opposite shore at dramatic heights. The weather was cooling and clouds now darkened what had previously been a sunny day. The cool weather and threat of rain calmed and soothed Mike as he abandoned his book and drank in the atmosphere.

Moments of quiet and beauty like this, particularly when far away from their California home, invariably caused Mike to reflect upon his life. His mind drifted over his family, his law practice, his friends, his health, his finances. As usual, he found shortcomings in his attention to investments, his failure to take every possible picture to preserve the memories of his children's youth, and his failure to communicate sufficiently with family and distant friends from college and law school. But as always, he quickly realized his general delight with virtually all aspects of his life. Now, at age forty, he had little, if any, of the self-doubt or lack of fulfillment often experienced by males reaching the threshold of middle age. The only really gnawing concern for Mike was the pressure to use those years of life allotted to him in the most fulfilling manner possible.

The clouds were now thick over the lake, and a summer rain began to fall. The raindrops were misty and light at first but soon began to fall more heavily. Mike grabbed his book and scooted inside from the balcony. Soon flashes of lightning were seen outside the window. Rumblings of thunder followed closely. The sights and sounds of a thunderstorm always reminded Mike of his youth in Nebraska, where thunderstorms were commonplace. The inner sense of catharsis and relief that Mike associated with thunderstorms again rushed over him like a wave splashing him with serenity.

"Hi!" said Susie as she came into the hotel room. She was flushed and excited as she entered. "Our new friends from Ireland are great—we've been playing backgammon and having drinks. Patrick is thirteen and Rachel is eleven and they are both very nice. And they have these great Irish accents. I told them I was going to come back to take a run with my dad, and they said, 'And why would you want to go out and drown yourself in the pouring rain?'"

Susie did her best to mimic the accent of her new friends and did a most creditable job, nicely catching the lilt and cadence of the speech she had heard.

"James is still playing backgammon with them. It was James and Patrick against Rachel and me. Only James and I just rolled the dice, since they know how to play, and we're just learning. James and Patrick won six straight games, so James thinks he's like this great backgammon player or something. Anyway, Dad, can we take our run?"

Susie, who was already an avid runner, looked plaintively at her father, "Please?"

"Sue, I was really looking forward to running, too, but we have serious lightning out there," her father replied. "Did you ever hear about Lee Trevino or those other golfers getting hit by lightning? Outside, running around trees in a lightning storm, is not the place to be. . . ."

"I thought you liked to run in the rain and that it was all cooling and everything?"

"Yes, sweetheart, but not in the lightning, which can be considerably less cooling."

"Okay," moped Susie, who then picked up the Michelangelo action figure and began twisting its arms and legs and head.

About twenty minutes later James came in and also began to talk about Patrick and Rachel. "They are very polite, Mom, and Patrick and I won eight straight games of backgammon!"

"It's Patrick who is playing," said Susie.

"We're both doing it," snapped James.

"Well, you two need to get dressed for dinner," said their mother, "since we have reservations in the main hotel at eight."

Once dressed in his tie and blazer, James realized he had not told Patrick and Rachel that it was his golden birthday. Feeling more and more at home in the new hotel and having been briefly at their room after backgammon, James decided he should go over and tell them immediately.

"I'm going to go tell Patrick and Rachel that it's my tenth birthday," James announced.

"Hey, wait a minute, Jamer," said his father, "we're headed out to dinner soon. And do you even know where their room is?"

"Sure," said James. "I visited it for a bit."

"Well, you'll see them at dinner probably," said Janet. "But you don't have time to see them now."

The main dining facility at the Villa d'Este is a spacious rectangular room with large retractable glass windows on three sides, providing a full view of the lake and the opposite shore from most of the room. The shore across the lake rose steeply into the sky and was blanketed by trees, villas, and green everywhere. Partially enshrouded by fog, the green contrasted sharply with the midnight blue of the lake.

James, Sue, Janet, and Mike were among the first patrons to arrive for dinner, and they were given a table adjacent to a window overlooking the lake and the northern grounds of the hotel. After their waiter brought wine for Mike and Janet and mineral water and a Coke for Sue and James, several birthday toasts were made.

"A toast to being ten, since that's a hell of a good age to be!" "A toast to Michelangelo and the other Ninja Turtles!" "A toast to Italy and spaghetti Bolognese!" "A toast to the Red Sox!"

All four diners seemed particularly pleased that the right joyous birthday spirit had been reached.

Then Sue said, "I see Patrick and Rachel."

Patrick, Rachel, and their older brother, who looked to be about twenty, and a man and woman likely to be their parents, were walking toward the restaurant across the northern grounds of the hotel, directly in front of the Monk table. Susie and James both waved. Rachel saw them and vigorously waved back with a smile. Rachel, Patrick, and family were soon seated two tables away from the Monks, also at a table next to the window overlooking the lake.

Dinner for the Monks proceeded as delightfully as it had begun, and the excellent food, service, and view relaxed everyone. James had just finished his pasta. He had chosen the local specialty most closely resembling spaghetti Bolognese, and he was feeling very satisfied. He had enjoyed a terrific golden birthday, in no small part because of the new friends he had made. But the family focus on his birthday at dinner was special, too, and James felt appropriately celebrated.

Suddenly James saw a waiter walking toward him with a cake with lighted candles on it. In fact, it was the very proper man who had greeted and seated them when they entered the dining room. James saw his mom and dad smile and saw the man with the cake coming directly toward him. In only slightly accented English, the maître d' wished James a happy birthday and placed the cake with the burning candles in front of him. James looked down at the cake and saw that it said "Happy Birthday, James" and had ten candles on it. Soon his parents, sister, and much of the sophisticated crowd in the restaurant were signing "Happy Birthday" to James. His first thought was, "How did the waiter know my name and that it was my golden birthday?" He soon realized that his parents had arranged it.

James beamed a smile as the singing ended. He then made a secret wish and blew out all ten candles with a single breath. Now his wish might come true. Mike then quietly asked the maître d' if he could cut not only four pieces of cake for their table, but also pieces for the children sitting two tables away. The maître d' smoothly assured him that it would be his pleasure. Soon, Rachel, Patrick, and their brother found pieces of cake in front of them. They smiled and waved a thank-you to the Monk table. For James, the special nature of his golden birthday had been acknowledged. He quietly basked in the glow of the moment.

January 2018

The Glory of the Bard—William Shakespeare

Peering into the Distant Mirror of the past, I recall my first experience with the Bard, William Shakespeare. I think it was sophomore year of high school, 1965 or so, when we read *Julius Caesar*. It was new, different, and not so easily understood. But the stabbing of Caesar in the forum, so bold and vivid, had a great impact on me and my fellow sophomores. And there were great speeches, like Mark Antony's "I come to bury Caesar, not to praise him"—maybe the best known line of irony in English literature. As you recall, Antony then rouses the citizens against the conspirators and defends the honor of Caesar. Some phrases, like the description of "yond Cassius" who has "a lean and hungry look" and "Beware the ides of March," had a resonance even to the youthful ear.

Two years later, in Mr. Kral's twelfth-grade English class, we were taught *Hamlet*, in much more detail and with far more understanding. I remember reading it with interest on the varsity basketball team's bus trip to Kearney (I was the twelfth man and rarely played). Some of these speeches were mesmerizing and somehow seemed familiar, like the "To be, or not to be" speech and the wonderful couplets, like:

The time is out of joint—O cursed spite,
That ever I was born to set it right!

and

Let Hercules himself do what he may,
The cat will mew and dog will have his day.

When one becomes familiar with sentences in which the word order is unusual, the meaning starts to become more clear. Also, the Shakespearean meter, blank verse, or iambic pentameter, with five iambs, provides a pleasing rhythm throughout: da DA, da DA, da DA, da DA, da Da. A soft syllable followed by a hard one, five times each line.

With Mr. Kral's influence, I grew fond of Shakespeare, and in college I majored in English literature. I grew to love Dickens and Shakespeare, along with Geoffrey Chaucer, whose work we learned in the original Middle English. I thought about going to graduate school to study English, but finally opted for law school.

During law school and for the next decade or so, I did so much legal reading that I had little energy for classic literature. But as the years passed, I returned to the writers I loved, from Dickens to Jane Austen to George Eliot and, of course, Shakespeare. I gained a renewed and even stronger appreciation for Shakespeare. In the late 1990s I reread most of the Shakespeare plays I had already read, as well as most of those I had not previously enjoyed. I was hooked. The more one reads, the easier the plays are to comprehend. And the real beauty is images, the meter, and the wisdom. At times, when I am reading, often aloud to myself to hear the meter, I think, "This is ridiculously beautiful. How can he have been so brilliant?"

Now, I give a "shameless self-serving praise" trigger warning. This renewed appreciation also caused me to write a play in the style of Shakespeare, *The Tragedy of Orenthal, Prince of Brentwood*, a play that tells the story of the O. J. Simpson murders. I was honored when it won one of eight "Outstanding Book of the Year" awards by the Independent Publisher Book Awards in 2014. It is available on the Amazon and Barnes & Noble websites.

But the focus of this little essay is the fear that the modern world will deem the Bard too difficult and not worth the effort. I am convinced that with a wee bit of effort, the words become clear, and the complex thoughts and ideas come tumbling forth. I see some colleges, including my own college and law school, Harvard and Penn, crumbling to the cries of a few that we should ignore the old, dead, white men and focus only upon diverse modern literature. This, in my view, is a horrible mistake. Embrace the new and the diverse, no question, but do not discard the past. I love Shakespeare not because he is male, or dead, or white, but because he is a genius. To see far lesser literary works drastically reduce the emphasis on the Bard is sad and a loss to all students. Isn't the point of scholarship to read the best that mankind has written?

Even more distressing is the nascent effort to rewrite the language of Shakespeare to make it more accessible. This is a far greater crime in my view even than brushing Shakespeare aside. We should not repaint the *Mona Lisa*, rescore Mozart's *Marriage of Figaro*, rebuild the Eiffel Tower, or revise the Gettysburg Address. And we should not rewrite the most beautiful language ever written. To destroy the meter, toss aside the metaphors, and "dumb down" the works of Shakespeare is neither wise nor necessary.

The prologue to *Romeo and Juliet* reads, verbatim, as follows:

Two households, both alike in dignity,
    In fair Verona, where we lay our scene,
From ancient grudge break to new mutiny,
    Where civil blood makes civil hands unclean.
From forth the fatal loins of these two foes
    A pair of star-crossed lovers take their life;
Whose misadventured piteous overthrows
    Doth with their death bury their parents' strife.
The fearful passage of their death-marked love,
    And the continuance of their parents' rage,
Which, but their children's end, nought could remove,
    Is now the two hours' traffic of our stage;
The which if you with patient ears attend,
What here shall miss, our toils shall strive to mend.

Is this really that impossible to comprehend? I think not. When you read the original Shakespeare with even a modicum of attention, it is not impenetrable. There will be an occasional word that will be footnoted to show the meaning in Elizabethan English, which may be different than the current meaning. But this is a small price to pay. The original, particularly when read out loud, has the pleasing meter, the iambic pentameter, and is lilting and calming somehow. The sonnet form in which it is written is also pleasing, with the rhyme scheme of: **ABAB CDCD EFEF** and **GG**.

Then compare a version of this prologue that is simplified to make it more accessible:

Our story takes place in Verona
    Involving two prominent families.
Longstanding disputes existed

Which broke out into new violence among citizens.
A romance between youths of the different families
    Ended when each committed suicide.
This tragic result and their deaths
    Ended the feud and brought peace.
The story of their love and death
    And the anger of each family,
Which ended only with their deaths,
    Is the story we tell today.
And if you listen closely
You will learn more details of this tale.

The simplification, which admittedly I myself wrote, is, by comparison, incredibly wanting. It lacks the rhythm of the meter and the comforting rhyme scheme of the sonnet form. It also lacks the more precise and expressive words, some of which are less frequently seen today.

So I encourage each of you to give the Bard a freaking chance. Pick a fun play to begin with, like *Romeo and Juliet* or *A Midsummer Night's Dream*. For just a bit of effort, you will be lavishly rewarded. And let us all revolt against the bastardization and simplification of the Bard's plays. Why change the best words ever written?

March 2018

The Joy of the Olympics

My daughter recently posted on Facebook a picture of my five-year-old grandson, Leonardo, and me, in our seats at a Minnesota Wild hockey game. Her comment, referring to her son and father, was, "The two most sports-obsessed people I know in their natural habitat." I proudly plead guilty to the charge. Sports have always been a joy for me, and not the least among my sporting passions is the Olympics.

I first became enthralled with the Olympics in 1960, at age eleven, when watching the Rome Olympics on our black-and-white television. I thrilled to the feats of the outrageous and completely likable Cassius Clay, the willowy speedster Wilma Rudolph, and the decathlete Rafer Johnson. These were a watershed Olympics, as is well chronicled in the recent book *Rome 1960: The Summer Olympics That Stirred the World*, by David Maraniss.

In early September 1960, just following the completion of the Rome Olympics, my friends and I created our own "Neighborhood Olympics." Most of the events occurred at Randy Speihs's house and the vacant lot across the street on 13th and Elm, just north of Howard School. Randy and I and our buddies George Ayoub, Craig Johnson, Mike Parmley, Van Coker, Billy Murphy, and others I don't recall precisely all participated. We had a one-hundred-yard dash and a four-hundred-yard race around the block. In the vacant lot we built a high jump and pole vault by putting a couple of two-by-four uprights in the ground, with nails in them to hold the bamboo crossbar. We held the high jump and the pole vault, using a bamboo vaulting pole. Fascinated by the techniques in the shot put, I had earlier that year bought an eight-pound shot put from Russell Sports, and we used that for the shot put event. As it turned out, my buddy George Ayoub later became the shot put star at Walnut and Senior. I also seem to recall we used an old hubcap for a discus. We also held bike races around the block.

Around this time, when I was eleven, I also recall mentally calculating whether I would be a senior in college in an Olympic year, since I knew it would be easier to make the Olympic basketball team as a senior, and that was clearly what I intended to do. I calculated that, alas, the Summer Olympics would be in 1968, when I was a college sophomore. Ah, sweet youth and sweet innocence.

My love of the Olympics never waned, and I was fortunate enough to attend in person both the Los Angeles Olympics in 1984 and the Sydney Olympics in 2000. At each of these two Olympics I splurged on track-and-field tickets, attending most evening sessions. In Los Angeles, I was able to see Joan Benoit at mile two of the marathon, which was on San Vicente Boulevard, a block and a half from our home in Santa Monica. Benoit won the gold medal in the first-ever Olympic women's marathon. I was also was able to see such stars as Carl Lewis, Sebastian Coe, and Mary Decker.

In Sydney, on Monday, September 25, 2000, I saw Michael Johnson win the four-hundred-meter gold medal and the famous indigenous Aussie Cathy Freeman win the gold medal for the home country in the women's four hundred meters. On that same September 25 night, I saw British jumper Jonathan Edwards win the men's triple jump; saw the first-ever women's pole vault competition, won by American Stacy Dragila; and watched a classic ten-thousand-meter race won by Haile Gebrselassie of Ethiopia over Paul Tergat of Kenya, in a photo finish. Later, the Bud Greenspan documentary on the Sydney Olympics called this night "The greatest night in track-and-field history."

As the years passed, I became more aware that politics often tainted the Olympics and made it less pristine. I was upset when the U.S. boycotted the 1980 Moscow Olympics (how could Carter strip athletes of the chance to participate, when many had been preparing their whole lives for this event?). I was also annoyed when the Russians then boycotted the 1984 Olympics.

But wonderful stories continued to occur in the Olympics, including the Franz Klammer downhill victory in 1976; the 1980 "Miracle on Ice" hockey game, when the U.S. upset the heavily favored Russians; the dominance of Eric Heiden and Bonnie Blair in speed skating; and a hundred more. And the addition of the snowboarding events brought a new exciting sport to the Winter Olympics.

So I was ready for this year's Winter Olympics in South Korea. I have found that I don't really get excited until the competition begins, and then I become hooked. This year's Olympics, like most, had troubling political issues, but I think it was an inspiring Olympics.

The International Olympic Committee purportedly banned Russia from these Olympics, since the IOC found that Russia had systematically engaged in doping and changing test samples. That certainly merited a ban. But it soon became clear is was not much of a ban. One hundred and sixty-eight Russian athletes were allowed to compete. While they could not use the Russian flag, they wore red, marched in as a team in the Opening Ceremonies, were allowed to have teams in hockey and other sports, and were listed as a team in the medal standings. While I had assumed the individuals would be referred to as something like "Unaffiliated Olympic Athletes," the team was called "Olympic Athletes from Russia." Some punishment. That name is as ridiculous as the name of baseball's "Los Angeles Angels of Anaheim." And to top it off, two of the "Olympic Athletes from Russia" tested positive for banned substances in South Korea.

But the Russians aside, these Olympics came off quite well, I think. I loved the fact that Norway, a less populous country, topped the medal standings. I loved that a snowboarder, Ester Ledecká, was the surprise winner in the super G Alpine event and was in such disbelief, she thought the scoreboard made a mistake. I enjoyed the commentary of Mike Tirico, Tara Lipinski, and the flamboyant Johnny Weir. I looked forward to the biathlon, the blend of cross-country skiing and shooting. Someone said the biathlon is like running a marathon and then, with heart pounding, having to thread a needle. My grandchildren would get down on the floor and pretend to shoot and then, if they missed, go around the room pretending to ski the penalty lap.

There were several wonderful moments in these Olympics that brought me great joy, great emotion, and a few tears, including the following:

Shaun White

The most dominant snowboarder in history, with golds in the half-pipe in both the 2006 and 2010 Games, White is the Godfather of Olympics Snowboarding. But White did not medal in the 2014 Games, and it looked like he might never again be on the podium.

Also, just this past October, he had a horrific training accident that required over twenty stitches on his face and put him in the hospital for a long stint. But here he was, more measured and wise than before, sounding actually quite intelligent, trying to recapture the magic at age thirty-one. In the final, he produced a terrific run that put him in first place going into the final runs. A dream come true. But a very talented Japanese boarder, Ayumu Hirano, then pulled off a spectacular run to take over the lead on the next-to-last run of the entire competition. White was now in second place with only one run left. But on his last run, under immense pressure and with no room for any glitch, White produced a run for the ages, with a high degree of difficulty and flawless execution. He had won the gold medal on his last run. Then we saw him immediately overcome by emotion, breaking into tears. He found his mother and hugged her, sobbing like a baby. I was thrilled and stunned by the magnificent performance, and I soon found myself a bundle of tears.

Lindsey Vonn and Mikaela Shiffrin

Lindsey Vonn has dominated Alpine skiing and the World Cup circuit for over a decade. She now has more World Cup victories than any woman in history. At age thirty-three, she was clearly in her last Olympics, and despite a nice run, she finished third to win the bronze medal in the downhill, her signature event. In her post-race interview, she poured out her heart's deepest feelings, expressing love of the competition and her sadness that this would be her last Olympics. She said she hoped her recently deceased grandfather would be proud of her bronze medal this last Olympics, then began to sob. And of course I began to cry also. I wanted to tell her, "Lindsey, you have been an amazing athlete who has dominated your sport and you have now medaled in the downhill at the geriatric age of thirty-three. You are the best female Alpine skier the world has ever seen. Of course your grandfather would be totally proud of you!"

Twenty-two-year-old Mikaela Shiffrin is the new Alpine legend, and she has stunned the World Cup circuit by winning most of the slalom races in the last three years. She also was very open and emotional in her interviews, expressing her love for the Olympics and her anxiety before races, often throwing up before a race. She did very well, winning gold in the giant slalom and the silver in the combined Alpine event. But in her specialty, the slalom, she finished fourth, not making the podium, and was crushed. But the next day, she posted a message saying essentially that while sometimes you win and sometimes you lose, the joy is being able to be part of such a wonderful competition and all the high stakes that are part of it. A very gracious remark from a wonderful young woman.

The U.S. Women's Hockey Team

Women's hockey in the Olympics has been dominated by the Canadians and the Americans. But after the U.S. won the gold in 1998, Canada won the next four golds, in 2002, 2006, 2010, and 2014. The U.S. lost a heartbreaker in 2014, leading 2-0 in the gold medal game but seeing the Canadians come back to beat them.

Both Canada and the U.S. made it to the gold medal game this Olympics, and it was one of the best hockey games I have ever seen. Played with skill and passion, it was a nail-biter. After the U.S. scored first, Canada scored two goals in the second period to go up 2-1. The third period was fascinating, with both teams coming close to scoring and the tension palpable. Finally, with less than ten minutes to play, the U.S. scored to tie the game at 2-2. After no scoring in the twenty-minute sudden-death overtime, the game was then decided on penalty shots. As individual women took penalty shots, each was painfully important, since any one shot could mean a gold medal. Tied after the required five shooters, the shootout also went overtime. On the sixth shooter, which now was sudden death, the U.S.'s Jocelyne Lamoureux-Davidson scored on an amazing shot involving three different fakes to put the U.S. up by one. Now it was up to our twenty-year-old goalie, Maddie Rooney, to stop the final Canadian shooter cold, and she did. USA wins!

The game was so close and tense that at the end, I jumped up, shouted, and thrust my fists in the air. I am told I was not the only one to do so. Then you saw an overwhelming scene of high emotion, with women on both teams in tears—tears of sadness for Canada and tears of joy for the USA. This sparkling game alone made this Olympics a resounding success for me.

U.S. Men's Curling

For the first time ever, I paid serious attention to the curling competition, and I learned a bit more about it. The U.S. men's gold medal was perhaps the biggest upset of the Olympics. The team had performed horribly at the 2014 Olympics and were dropped by the U.S. federation that supports curling teams. But these men continued on their own dime and surprised everyone by making it back to the Olympics in 2018. After a horrible start this year, losing four of their first six games, they found magic. They won three straight matches to make the medal round and then won the last two games to grab the gold medal. A group of men in their twenties and thirties from Minnesota and Wisconsin, they did not appear particularly athletic; indeed, they seemed a bit frumpy. But they played with extraordinary skill. To see them singing the national anthem with gusto at their gold medal ceremony was a joy.

Jessie Diggins and Kikkan Randall

My final feel-good story was Jessie Diggins's and Kikkan Randall's gold medal in the women's cross-country skiing team sprint. This was the first-ever Olympic medal for the U.S. in cross-country skiing. The finish was also mesmerizingly close. Diggins came from third place in the last two hundred meters, passed the other two teams, and crossed the line about a foot ahead of her nearest opponent. Once again, joy and tears erupted. The entire women's cross-country team made a name for itself even before the gold, with their smiles and spirited embrace of the Olympics. Diggins was chosen to be the flag bearer for the U.S. in the Closing Ceremonies, and she could not stop smiling.

So farewell, Olympics, for a couple of years. Many of this year's memories will stick with us for some time.

May 2018

Susannah's Boston Marathon and a Trip to Fenway

The initial reflection in today's Distant Mirror is from 1967. That September, after graduating from GI Senior High, my mother and grandmother, with tears in their eyes, drove me to Omaha, where I boarded a United flight and flew to Boston for my freshman year at Harvard College.

This was a day of many firsts for me: the first time I ever flew in an airplane, the first time I was ever east of the Mississippi, and, as our plane landed near the Atlantic, the first time I ever saw an ocean. After getting settled in my dorm room, on the same night, I joined a group of fellow freshmen and took the subway (another first) to Fenway Park to see the Boston Red Sox play the Kansas City Athletics. This was a huge first, the first Major League Baseball game I ever attended. A few weeks later, I snuck into the first game of the World

Series and saw Bob Gibson and the St. Louis Cardinals defeat my new favorite team, the Red Sox. A lifelong Red Sox love affair had begun. The first cut is the deepest.

In 1967, I fell in love not only with the Red Sox, but also with Harvard, the Boston area, and, in the spring, the Boston Marathon. Until 1968, the Boston Marathon was run on April 19, Patriots' Day, which is also my late mother's birthday. (Since 1969 Patriots' Day and the Boston Marathon have been held on the third Monday in April.) On Marathon Monday there is also an early Red Sox game that begins at 11:00 a.m. The game generally ends just as the first marathon runners go by Fenway Park, at mile twenty-five of the course. I learned that the Boston Marathon is one of the oldest and, arguably, the most prestigious marathon in the world. A runner must run a very challenging qualifying time to run Boston, and only about the top 10 percent of all marathoners now qualify.

My junior year at Harvard, I met Janet Bogle, also a junior at nearby Wellesley College. This August will mark our forty-fourth wedding anniversary. In April of my senior year I joined Janet and some of her friends at Wellesley to watch the marathon runners pass. We dressed up as mythological figures and cheered the runners as they passed the fourteen-mile mark. I think I wore some sort of stupid toga or something. Decades later, my daughter, Susannah, also attended Wellesley College, and amazingly, in 1998, she lived in the same dorm, Munger Hall, in which her mother had lived twenty-seven years earlier. So in April 1998, I watched the marathon with Susannah, in front of the same Wellesley dorm, and the crowd was even larger and more vocal than twenty-seven years earlier. The cheering Wellesley crowd has become so massive and loud they now call it the "Wellesley Tunnel" of sound.

In the 1980s I began to run some 5Ks and 10Ks to try to stay in shape. In 1986, Susannah, who was born in Boston in 1976, just before Janet and I moved to California, began to run with me. She became a very successful competitive runner, captain of both her high school and Wellesley College cross-country teams. She had been entered in the 1998 Boston Marathon by the Wellesley cross-country coach, but she was unable to run due to an injury. For the next twenty years, she regretted not running Boston, and it became her mission in life to qualify for the race and run it. Her husband, Caesar, qualified and ran it in 2016, and then in 2017, after much hard work, Susannah also qualified, and ran a three-hour, thirty-one-minute marathon as a forty-one-year-old. She was ecstatic! This year, 2018, both Susannah and Caesar qualified to run the Boston Marathon. She would fulfil one of her lifetime dreams and run it with her husband.

So two weeks ago, Janet and I went to Boston with Susannah and Caesar and our grandchildren Victoria and Leo, along with my cousin Randy Garroutte (GISH class of 1970) and Randy's daughter Erica and his son-in-law John, to root on Susannah and Caesar.

The six days in Boston were a total joy. We got lots of time with our seven-year-old granddaughter, Victoria, and our five-year-old grandson, Leo. Our hotel had a pool, so Grandpa Mike went swimming with Victoria and Leo on three separate days. On the Sunday before the marathon, we swam for about three hours. Among the wonderful moments was when Victoria met a boy her age and they were swimming together, racing and goofing around. She soon came over to me and said, "Grandpa, I think that boy likes me." At dinner that night, the boy and his family were at the table next to ours, and when Victoria and the boy saw each other, they each gave a big wave.

Another highlight was when I took Leo to his first Fenway Park game on Saturday. My college buddy Tom Werner, now one of the Red Sox owners, got us seats on the field level in the very front row, just four seats to the left of the Sox dugout. Leo had a wonderful time, was given a ball from the clubhouse by an usher, and even chatted with the Red Sox mascot. Leo is at a stage where he asks everyone, including complete strangers, how old they are. The mascot, from inside his costume, said that he was twenty. Leo had a light lunch of popcorn, a hot dog, peanuts, an apple, french fries, frozen lemonade, and hot chocolate. After the game, the loudspeaker blared out "Dirty Water," by The Standells (you know the song, "I love that dirty water / Oh, Boston, you're my home"). Leo was so pumped that he was dancing big-time as we walked out, and about twenty people were smiling at this bold little dancer. All day long Leo kept telling strangers that Fenway Park was the oldest baseball park in the majors. And he proudly told every stranger, "My mom and dad are *both* running the marathon."

The marathon itself was wonderful and horrible. Horrible since it was run in a total monsoon, in a temperature of about thirty-eight degrees, into a twenty-five-mile-per-hour headwind. It would rain steadily, then totally pour buckets for twenty minutes, then lighten up, and then pour even more heavily. It never stopped raining all day. Over one hundred runners ended up in the hospital with hypothermia and other problems. About fifty dropped out in Wellesley at the halfway mark and went to the Methodist church for warmth and food. Janet and I and the kids and cousin Randy, Erica, and John stationed ourselves at mile twenty-four, in Coolidge Corner (two blocks from the apartment we lived in when Susannah was born). We watched for a half hour or so and were miserable. The wind was messing with our umbrellas, we were soaked, and Victoria said the water in her shoes had turned warm from her body heat.

So we retreated to a nearby Peet's Coffee and hung out there for an hour, watching Susannah and Caesar's progress on our runner-tracking apps. We went back out about twenty minutes before Sue was supposed to go by, saw her, and even got a picture. She looked very wet but surprisingly fresh. Caesar ran with Sue for most of the race, but he had bathroom problems and eventually Sue went on ahead of him.

And the wonderful part of the marathon is that they both finished. Sue was euphoric. She said the race was so hard that she considered quitting many times. She told herself that she would never have to run another marathon and that she had to finish. But after finishing and getting the medal and the hundreds of Facebook congratulations and love, she said she was already planning for another Boston Marathon. Caesar, a true gazelle, whose personal record is two hours, fifty-eight minutes, and who has run maybe sixteen marathons, said it was the most miserable race of his life. I am very proud of them both. This was a lifetime goal for Susannah, a native Bostonian, and it was so satisfying to see it come true.

Boston, the Red Sox, Fenway Park, and the Boston Marathon are all very special to me from my days at Harvard and thereafter. So a weekend that combined my grandchildren, Fenway Park, the Red Sox, and my own flesh and blood making a dream come true by completing the Boston Marathon was as good as it gets.

July 2018

Ten (or Fifteen) Favorite Books of All Time

Our past reflections from the Distant Mirror (to keep the metaphor going) have touched upon my love of books and literature. I shared my memories of going to the Carnegie Library on 2nd Street with my buddy Steve Schroeder in third grade or so and checking out the maximum of six books each. My childhood was blessed by reading not only every sports book in sight but also the great *Tom Sawyer* and *Huckleberry Finn*, the charming Chip Hilton sports books of Clair Bee, and the heartwarming stories of Beverly Cleary, including *Henry Huggins* and *Beezus and Ramona*.

Katherine Martin (née Katherine Langdon), my beloved second-grade teacher at Howard School, brought the Beverly Clearly books into my life. In an earlier Distant Mirror column about the teachers I most treasured, I mentioned Miss Martin, who so greatly inspired me not only to read, but to love reading. One of the most rewarding parts of writing this column is that it has allowed me to reconnect with old friends. The most emotional for me was reconnecting with Katherine "Kass" Martin in this past year. After she read my newsletter, her friend Jane Richardson gave me her contact information, and I wrote her with my thanks and fond memories. Later we spoke on the phone and shared many memories from her 1957 second-grade class. Kass was as charming and positive as ever, and speaking with her these sixty-two years later was a thrill.

The value of reading is universally acknowledged. One of the most common habits of very successful people is continuing to read voraciously through their lifetime. Many very successful persons, from Warren Buffett to Bill Gates to Mark Zuckerberg, read prodigious numbers of books on a regular basis. To read the best that has been written delights and surprises. It shocks and amazes. It warms and mellows. And it is invaluable when watching *Jeopardy!* Some of my most euphoric moments in life have been while reading in my easy chair, or at the pool, or with a glass of iced tea on the patio. The well-read person not only learns the lessons taught by great literature but also has a pleasing hobby to soothe the tired soul for the rest of one's life. The most poignant parts of my top fifteen list below have brought me to tears.

The great educator Jacques Barzun, in his book *Teacher in America*, emphasized that everything we read has value, ending with a favorite line of mine—even "Trash is excellent." I agree. But over the years I have come to ask, "Why not read the classics primarily, the best that has been thought and written?" There is a wonderful book by Harold Bloom called *How to Read and Why*. The title is a bit misleading, but it is essentially a list of wonderful books, some well-known classics and some not, that will reward the reader greatly. I once discussed this book with a law partner, who asked if such lists are not "elitist." Well, the answer is no, since anyone can read them and all will benefit.

In this spirt of selecting wonderful books to read, after my fiftieth GIHS reunion last year, a few of my close friends from the class of 1967 and I set out to record and share our "Favorite Books of All Time" in top ten lists, reminiscent of David Letterman. I found these fascinating, and hereby share them with you. Please note that we agreed not to include Shakespeare, since his works would dominate any list. He is the King, the Bard, the most eloquent writer in the English language.

We all had trouble keeping the list to ten books. My longtime pal Jeff Greenberger was particularly obstreperous and refused to reduce his list to even twenty. But, with a little editing, here are our lists of ten . . . or fifteen.

JEFF GREENBERGER:

1. *Ulysses*, by James Joyce
2. *One Hundred Years of Solitude*, by Gabriel García Márquez
3. *All the Pretty Horses*, by Cormac McCarthy
4. *Crossing to Safety*, by Wallace Stegner
5. *War and Peace*, by Leo Tolstoy
6. *David Copperfield*, by Charles Dickens
7. *Lolita*, by Vladimir Nabokov
8. *Middlemarch*, by George Eliot
9. *The Adventures of Augie March*, by Saul Bellow
10. *Winnie-the-Pooh*, by A. A. Milne
11. *Swann's Way*, by Marcel Proust
12. *The Satanic Verses*, by Salman Rushdie
13. *Love Medicine*, by Louise Erdrich
14. *Death in Venice*, by Thomas Mann
15. *Cloud Atlas*, by David Mitchell

DENNIS HICKSTEIN:

1. *War and Peace*, by Leo Tolstoy
2. *Ulysses*, by James Joyce

3. *The Brothers Karamazov,* by Fyodor Dostoevsky
4. *David Copperfield,* by Charles Dickens
5. *The Great Gatsby,* by F. Scott Fitzgerald
6. *For Whom the Bell Tolls,* by Ernest Hemingway
7. *The Sound and the Fury,* by William Faulkner
8. *To the Lighthouse,* by Virginia Woolf
9. *A Death in the Family,* by James Agee
10. *Raise High the Roof Beam, Carpenters*; *and Seymour: An Introduction,* by J. D. Salinger
11. *Look Homeward, Angel,* by Thomas Wolfe
12. *Crossing to Safety,* by Wallace Stegner
13. *The Alexandria Quartet,* by Lawrence Durrell
14. *All the King's Men,* by Robert Penn Warren
15. *Heart of Darkness,* by Joseph Conrad

THOMAS MEEDEL:

1. *Walden,* by Henry David Thoreau
2. *Cancer Ward,* by Aleksandr Solzhenitsyn
3. *Crime and Punishment,* by Fyodor Dostoevsky
4. *To Kill a Mockingbird,* by Harper Lee
5. *Jude the Obscure,* by Thomas Hardy
6. *Don Quixote,* by Miguel de Cervantes
7. *Cannery Row,* by John Steinbeck
8. *Hiroshima,* by John Hersey
9. *Adventures of Huckleberry Finn,* by Mark Twain
10. *On the Origin of Species,* by Charles Darwin

JAMES VOHLAND:

1. *Charlotte's Web,* by E. B. White
2. The James Bond books, by Ian Fleming
3. *Slaughterhouse-Five,* by Kurt Vonnegut
4. *Lucifer's Hammer,* by Jerry Pournelle and Larry Niven
5. Charlie Chan series, by Earl Derr Biggers

6. *Portnoy's Complaint*, by Philip Roth
7. *Red Sky at Morning*, by Richard Bradford
8. *I Shall Not Be Moved*, by Maya Angelou
9. *To Kill a Mockingbird*, by Harper Lee
10. *The Bell Jar*, by Sylvia Plath
11. *Andersonville*, by MacKinlay Kantor
12. *The Devil in the White City*, by Erik Larson
13. *Lord of the Flies*, by William Golding
14. All books by Janet Evanovich
15. *Jack Reacher*, by Lee Child

MICHAEL MONK:

1. *War and Peace*, by Leo Tolstoy
2. *The Pickwick Papers*, by Charles Dickens
3. *Middlemarch*, by George Eliot
4. *Tom Jones*, by Henry Fielding
5. *Huckleberry Finn*, by Mark Twain
6. *To Kill a Mockingbird*, by Harper Lee
7. *The Canterbury Tales*, by Geoffrey Chaucer (original Middle English version)
8. *East of Eden*, by John Steinbeck
9. *The Magic Mountain*, by Thomas Mann
10. *Pride and Prejudice*, by Jane Austen
11. *A Tale of Two Cities*, by Charles Dickens
12. *Robinson Crusoe*, by Danial Defoe
13. *The Stand*, by Stephen King
14. *Tortilla Flat*, by John Steinbeck
15. *The Big Sleep*, by Raymond Chandler

If anyone has a need for a summer reading suggestion, you could do worse than trying any book on these lists.

September 2018

The Wonderful Books of Beverly Cleary

It is July 1959, 10:00 a.m. on a muggy Tuesday morning in Grand Island. A mildly ragged but enthusiastic group of five boys aged eleven or twelve, some wearing only swimsuits, are riding their bikes south to the Platte River, to swim, goof around, and perhaps try to spear some fish. Having told their mothers what they were up to, they took off, promising only to be home by dinner. No carefully packed lunches had been prepared, no admonitions were given about sunscreen, and in general the boys were on their own. They were told to be careful. Later that day they returned and worked outside on the wooden fort they were building in one of the boys' backyards.

The next day most of the Howard enrollment was at the Summer Shows at the Grand Theatre. For one dollar you got to see eight movies over the summer. Most children walked to the Grand Theatre on their own. That night, a few of the boys rode their bikes to Grace Abbott Park for their Little League game. Many of the boys' parents would arrive later by car, but some parents did not attend, and their boys were fine on their own.

The following day, Thursday, saw many of these friends again riding their bikes to the municipal pool, unattended by parents and swimming all day. Many days that summer started with a 9:00 a.m. pickup baseball game at Howard School. Self-organized, no adults part of it, and played with gusto by young baseball fanatics.

It was not exactly Tom Sawyer, although similar in many ways. But it was ultimately better, since despite the freedom given children, the parents were assiduously conscious of just what the boys and girls did and were very loving in their direction. What a way to engender confidence, independence, and audacity in the youth.

I hope the Grand Island of 2018 has retained some of this small-town flavor. Despite the avalanche of modern technology, the growth of the city, and the simple reality of changing times, I think the geography and culture of Grand Island and general trustworthiness of most Midwestern folks will always provide a bit of that life. But I am sure that parents today are more circumspect and less trusting. I also wonder if it was that moment in time or the geography and culture of Grand Island that made this life possible. My college roommate, Steve Sicher, grew up in the 1950s in Manhattan, the heart of New York City. Yet even as a boy of six or seven years old, he rode a public bus by himself to his private grammar school. So I suppose both the era and the location are factors.

Middle-class American life in the 1950s and 1960s is wonderfully captured by the books of Beverly Cleary, who is adept at describing how a young child thinks, what motivates that child, and how the child perceives the world around him or her. She published her first book, *Henry Huggins*, in 1950, and at the time of this writing, she is still alive, at 102 years young. [Cleary has since passed away, in

October 2021, at the age of 104.] I have mentioned her in this column before, since I have been a lifelong fan. She wrote books that are mostly directed at beginning readers, or those aged five to eleven or so. The heroes are Henry Huggins, his dog Ribsy, and his neighbors Beezus Quimby and her little sister Ramona Quimby. Ramona, ultimately the most captivating character of all, is a total delight, and I am no less fond of her because my late mother was named Ramona. I loved the Beverly Cleary books when I was seven, in Mrs. Kass Martin's second-grade class, I loved them in college, I loved reading them to my children, and I love reading them to my grandchildren today. I was recently reading *Henry Huggins* to my five-year-old grandson and eight-year-old granddaughter. While at first uninterested, they quickly became entranced. My grandson had to go to the bathroom and, being a child of the video age, said to me, breathlessly, interrupting my reading, "Grandpa, can you pause it while I go to the bathroom?"

Cleary's first book, *Henry Huggins*, tells the story of Henry Huggins, a third-grade boy who lives in Portland, Oregon, in a typical middle-class family. Henry finds a stray skinny dog, names him "Ribsy," and convinces his parents to let him keep the mutt. Henry is required to feed and care for Ribsy, and Ribsy hangs with him and even is allowed to run loose and wait for Henry under a large tree at the school playground. Henry bonds with Ribsy, and Ribsy immediately makes Henry's life much more interesting.

Three scenes from the book vividly display the tenor of the times and the values of the 1950s.

The Bus Ride: The very day Henry finds Ribsy and gives him a home, he is forced to take his new pooch home on a municipal bus. But during the bus ride, Ribsy gets away from Henry, bumping into a lady, who spills all her groceries, leaving apples on the bus aisle, on which a heavyset man stumbles and falls. Bodies and groceries are strewn everywhere, and the man is left unceremoniously sitting on his bottom in the aisle. In short, all heck breaks loose. But what happens? Do the grown-ups shout at Henry and berate him? Do threats or profanity ensue? No. After a moment of befuddlement and surprise, the man in the aisle begins to laugh at the havoc that he sees around him. Soon everyone on the bus is laughing out loud. Would this happen today? I hope so.

The Lost Football: Henry's older friend Scooter McCarthy, a fifth grader, had received a new football for his birthday. It was a good one, a "genuine cowhide leather" one that smelled wonderful and had that solid thump when you patted it or caught it. While playing catch with Scooter, Henry accidently throws the ball into the open window of a passing car. The car's driver speeds on, not stopping. Then, immediately, Scooter demands that Henry buy him a new ball. Henry does not dispute his obligation, but instead tries to figure out how to raise enough money to buy Scooter a ball. Henry proceeds to liquidate all of his assets but is still woefully short of the thirteen dollars the ball costs.

But Henry discovers he can make money catching night crawlers, since his fishing fanatic neighbor agrees to pay him one cent for each worm. This means, however, that Henry has to find over 1,000 night crawlers to pay his debt. His parents allow him to go to the nearby park, after dark, by himself, for hours. Finally, they join him and help him catch the necessary 1,000 worms. The parents never once suggest that Henry should not have to pay for the football, and they never once offer to pay for him. They are struggling middle-class parents. So Henry obtains the necessary money. But before he can buy the ball for Scooter, a stranger appears at the Hugginses' front door. It is the stranger into whose car the ball had been thrown. He apologizes for his delay in returning the ball and explains that he was driving his sick wife to the hospital and could not stop.

So Henry does the right thing and is rewarded by ultimately having enough money now to buy his own football.

Whose Dog Is It? This is the most telling, most poignant, and best scene in the book. I recently had to hide my tears reading it to my grandchildren. Near the end of *Henry Huggins*, Henry and his friend Beezus, her sister Ramona, and their friend Robert, all but Ramona in the third grade, are playing in the front yard. The older Scooter McCarthy, in the fifth grade, comes riding by on his bike and stops to chat.

Just then an even older boy, maybe fourteen, rides up on his bike. Henry's dog, Ribsy, seeing the strange boy, starts barking like crazy. The boy stops and calls to Ribsy, "Dizzy, hey Dizzy, Dizzy." Soon Ribsy runs to the boy for a joyful reunion, since the boy had been Ribsy's original owner. The boy explains that Ribsy escaped from a dog sitter when the boy and his family were on vacation. Since Ribsy had shed his collar and license, there was no way for the boy to find his dog, and no way for Henry to identify the owner.

Henry has now cared for Ribsy going on two years. He had spent money on the dog, but more importantly, it was his dog, and he liked his dog. The other boy said he would pay for the expenses Henry incurred in caring for "Dizzy," but that Dizzy was really his dog and had been so since the dog was a puppy. So did this older boy simply grab Ribsy and ride away? No. Indeed, he understood how Henry felt. Henry's friends also came to his defense and now praised Ribsy, for the first time ever. But even they understood how the older boy must feel as well.

So on the spot, this group of kids, from ages five to fourteen, decided how to resolve the matter. They agreed to let the dog decide. Henry and the strange boy each stood on the sidewalk, about forty feet apart. They then placed "Ribsy/Dizzy" in the middle, and both boys were allowed to call the dog. Whichever boy Ribsy/Dizzy selected would be the owner. Scooter agreed to supervise the contest. The importance of this contest cannot be exaggerated.

After Scooter said "Go," both boys yelled wildly, calling Ribsy to come to them. At first Ribsy just yawned and sat down. Then Ribsy went about halfway to Henry, then stopped and scratched a flea. The strange boy now called out "Ribsy" instead of "Dizzy," which

Scooter ruled to be permissible. Finally Ribsy went the remaining distance to Henry and nestled up at Henry's feet. Ribsy had chosen Henry. All agreed this was fair, and after Henry agreed the boy could come and play with Ribsy whenever he wanted, the boy rode away.

There were no screaming matches, no threats, no resort to adults, no police involvement, no lawyer demands. Yet justice was served. Would this possibly happen today? Again, I very much hope so.

So if you have children or grandchildren, or if you yourself (like me) simply enjoy a great children's book, I cannot highly enough recommend the books of Beverly Cleary.

Lists of Favorite Books

My column in the last newsletter setting forth the favorite books lists compiled by my class of 1967 buddies and me drew little response. I did, however, receive a wonderful list of top twenty from my pal and fellow newsletter scribe and editor, George Ayoub. George's list is as follows:

1. *To Kill a Mockingbird*, by Harper Lee
2. *A Tale of Two Cities*, by Charles Dickens
3. *The Adventures of Huckleberry Finn*, by Mark Twain
4. *Shoeless Joe*, by W. P. Kinsella
5. *Catch-22*, by Joseph Heller
6. *The Grapes of Wrath*, by John Steinbeck
7. *The Monkey Wrench Gang*, by Edward Abbey
8. *Tess of the d'Urbervilles*, by Thomas Hardy
9. *A Clockwork Orange*, by Anthony Burgess
10. *Slaughterhouse-Five*, by Kurt Vonnegut
11. *A Confederacy of Dunces*, by John Kennedy Toole
12. *The Catcher in the Rye*, by J. D. Salinger
13. *The Brief Wondrous Life of Oscar Wao*, by Junot Díaz
14. *Boy's Life*, by Robert McCammon

15. *Heart of Darkness*, by Joseph Conrad
16. *The Killer Angels*, by Michael Shaara
17. *The Prince of Tides*, by Pat Conroy
18. *Les Misérables*, by Victor Hugo
19. *A Christmas Carol*, by Charles Dickens
20. *On the Road*, by Jack Kerouac

Happy reading.

November 2018

Leonardo's Love of Sports: Genetics or Environment?

Scientists, psychologists, and many others, for millennia, including such notable scholars as the Duke brothers in the movie *Trading Places*, have questioned whether the behavior of a person stems more from genetics or environment. Is it the DNA our parents gave us that inevitably will determine the general path we take, or the loving touch of a grandmother and gentle guidance about how to live life that more influence our life choices?

I am currently fascinated by this issue because of my five-year-old grandson, Leonardo. I will freely admit, and have in this column, that I am an avid sports fan. Some in my family would even say sports obsessed. Now mind you, I have many lifelong passions—including literature, theater, travel, exercise, history, and, beginning in college, art, ballet, and opera—and I continue to pursue them to this day.

But from the time I was a small boy, I have always been fascinated by the batted ball, the touchdown pass, the hundred-meter winner in the Olympics, the shooting guard in basketball who passes like a wizard, and the grace, shot blocking, and defense of the great Bill Russell. I wanted to watch any sport on television and play all sports in their season. My fellow scribe George Ayoub and I, and our friend Bobby McFarland, were playing baseball in the street as six-year-olds. I remember first understanding the concept of an average when, at about age seven, I noticed that Mickey Mantle's batting average had gone down. How could that happen? At about age seven my friend Steve Schroeder gave me about twenty old issues of *Sports Illustrated*, my first contact with the magazine. I treated them like they were as precious as the Dead Sea Scrolls, or an original copy of the U.S. Constitution, caressing them lovingly and examining each one in detail. I played Little League and Little Bigger League Baseball and one year with the American Legion Midgets. I participated in football, basketball, and track at Walnut Junior High and in high school. I was the sports editor of the *Islander* in both my junior and senior years, and in my junior and senior years of college, I was the sports director of the Harvard radio station, WHRB. I was the color commentator for our Harvard football broadcasts.

This has led to a life that begins each day with the sports section and involves multiple fantasy leagues at all times of the year and attendance at major sporting events whenever possible. From 1990 to 1994, my wife and I were minority owners of the San Diego Padres, a wonderful experience that went well beyond my wildest dreams when growing up in modest circumstances.

So when my two children were born, friends noted that I would now have them to share my sporting passion. And while my children enjoyed sports, it went in a slightly different direction. My daughter fell in love with running and swimming and liked many Olympic sports. She was a captain of her high school and college cross-country teams and this past year completed the Boston Marathon. But she was so-so on team sports. My son is also a big fan of auto racing, skiing, and shooting, but also not a huge fan of team sports.

Then came my grandson, Leonardo, who will be six on November 20. At the age of two, he was fascinated by his father's soccer balls. He learned to kick with the instep, with power and grace, at age three. He was playing in youth soccer games at age four, and he was warned in preschool not to kick the soccer ball, since he might hurt somebody. Every time he saw me watching a sport, he would join and ask questions about the play and who was winning. At age five, he now has his mom (my daughter) read the sports page to him every day. He watches soccer with his father and quickly became an avid fan of European soccer and the World Cup. He knows that Cristiano Ronaldo left the Spanish club Real Madrid to play for Juventus in Italy. He knows his uncle Ricardo loves Inter Milan in the Italian Serie A. He knows that Luka Modrić of Real Madrid is from Croatia. He knows that Harry Kane is the star striker for Tottenham Hotspur. Tottenham, by the way, is the only sports team I know named after a Shakespearian character (Harry Hotspur from *Henry IV, Part 1*). And he loves Leo Messi of Barcelona, as they share the name Leo.

Since they live in Minneapolis, he is already a fan of the Twins (several shirts and hats), the Vikings (several shirts), the Wild, the Timberwolves, and the MLS team, the Minnesota United Loons (a shirt and a hat). My eight-year-old granddaughter, Victoria, can do a perfect rendition of the sound of the loon at the games. Leo and I have gone together to about eight Twins games, a Wild game, a Red Sox game in Fenway Park, a UCLA basketball game in L.A., and a Minnesota Gophers vs. Nebraska Cornhuskers women's volleyball match a couple of weeks ago in Saint Paul. When at these games, he is totally engaged. He follows the score, asks about rules, and lives and dies with each play. For Halloween, he is going as the Vikings quarterback, Kirk Cousins, and already has his helmet, football, and Cousins jersey ready to go.

He loves to be with me in my Minnesota house's "man cave," where I have (1) a big-screen TV, (2) a street hockey net, with hockey sticks and a soft puck, and (3) a small basketball hoop attached to one wall. We play hockey, basketball, and Wiffle ball in the man cave. Sports are not only permitted but encouraged. The minute he and his sister arrive for a sleepover or visit, he says, "Grandpa, let's go down to the basement." He will often ask to watch some sport, and I have a trove of games recorded, so we watch. But while watching he simultaneously plays the sport himself, mimicking the actions, moves, and facial expressions of the players on the screen. He runs, jumps, and falls as the players do on television. He does a great imitation of a soccer player who is fouled and pretends to be dying.

He will at times declare he is playing in a game. "Grandpa, this is Las Vegas Golden Knights versus Minnesota Wild." He will then keep imaginary scores and make up imaginary players. "And Martin Flea scores for the Wild, his tenth goal of the game!" Martin Flea?

Earlier this year, my wife took our granddaughter for an afternoon outing while Leo and I stayed home. When they left, Leo said to me with a smile on his face, "Now we can watch whatever sports we want, Grandpa." He started kindergarten in September, and his teacher laughingly told his parents at the first teacher conference about Leo on the playground. She said he would describe the action on the playground in his sports announcer voice: "Oh, Jeremy just fell down for the third time during recess! Oh boy, that's got to hurt!"

For Christmas last year I got him a set of miniature helmets with the logos of every National Football League team. He played with them constantly, already recognizing most of the teams. He would also have imaginary games with the helmets. "Grandpa, it is Jaguars 23, Bears 5."

His love for sports helped him to begin to learn to read even before he entered kindergarten. He will ask me to pull out my iPhone and go over the scoreboard of recent games in every sport. A couple of weeks ago we checked all the scores from pro football, college football, the National Hockey League, the English Premier League soccer league, the Italian Serie A soccer league, the Spanish La Liga, Major League Soccer, and even the Big Ten women's volleyball scores. He would look at the scores and say, for example, "Ohhhh . . . Alabama beat some other team 65 to 31!" I was once recording a major soccer game between two English teams, Liverpool and Chelsea, while we were having lunch at a restaurant. Leo knew I was recording, but from halfway across a big restaurant, he saw the scroll underneath the game being shown on television and said, "OOOOH, Grandpa, bad news, Chelsea 2, Liverpool 1, and it is over!" I could barely read the words, but he had it down.

In addition, either sports has given him in an interest in numbers, or his fascination with numbers has increased his interest in sports. But he is acutely conscious of numbers and scores. Last June, when he and I watched the Golden State Warriors play the Cleveland Cavaliers in the NBA finals, he would say, "Grandpa, Warriors leading 43 to 35 . . . we are up eight points!" And he can tell you to this day the final score of last year's Viking–Eagles game, which the Eagles won to put them in the Super Bowl.

He has also developed an increased interest in geography arising from sports. As he closely watched the World Cup soccer results this past summer, he wanted to know where Brazil, Croatia, and Belgium were on the map. He already knew where the U.S., Mexico, Guatemala, England, France, and Russia were.

There is another interesting aspect of Leonardo's love of sports. My daughter, Susannah, has made it clear that he will not be permitted to play tackle football, due to the serious concussion and other injury risks involved. I strongly support this decision. Indeed, so does Leo, who, after mimicking the moves of a wide receiver making a catch, will then declare to me, "You know, Grandpa, football is very dangerous, and I like to watch, but I won't play tackle football." Finally, Leo has a tremendous characteristic that not all athletes have. If he fails at something—misses the Wiffle ball, does not make the basket, or shoots wide of the goal—he is unfazed. He does not get angry or discouraged but is always ready for more.

To return to genetics or environment, I personally think both play major roles in who we are. I know many friends and acquaintances who gained a love of sports, or opera, or art from a close relative or friend, from their environment. But reflecting on Leo, I have to think that the truly passionate sports fan, the one who lives and breathes the stuff, is that way in large part due to genetics. As Susannah has said more than once with Leo and me, "It skips a generation!" I think she is right.

As a final word, I type this after just returning from Boston, where I saw games one and two of this year's World Series. My beloved Red Sox had a great year. In part to annoy me and see my reaction, Leo rooted for the Dodgers. He points out that he was born in L.A., so I cannot argue. But for me, the beauty is that he cares.

January 2019

Adages I Live By

Over the years I have identified many simple adages (proverbs? words of wisdom? good practices? barnyard bromides?) that seem to help me make wise decisions. I will discuss just a few of these that I find interesting and of value. I do not pretend they are particularly original or necessarily involve complex thinking, but to me they are good habits:

First Things First

Of course, first things first. Who could dispute this? But just what are the "first things?" We all have a series of tasks or pleasures we intend to, or must, complete. The successful person in life carefully assesses which should come first. Some choices are easy. Should I put out the fire in the wastebasket before I finish reading the sports section? Some are less easy. Should I clean out the garage or go to the gym to exercise? Should I do my holiday shopping early or see the movie I have been thirsting to see, which leaves town tomorrow?

Some involve a more complicated analysis of what is more beneficial in the short run or the long run, what will bring me more happiness, and what task can be successfully completed, as opposed to the task that will plague you and likely not be doable. Many "firsts" are to eliminate serious risks if the task is not done. Hope for the best, but plan for the worst.

Some choices involve balancing the values of the person making the decision. Should I leave work early to see my daughter run in the cross-country meet, or spend time finishing the project at work that needs to be done soon. For me, the value of the experience of watching my daughter run had a high personal value. The moments of our lives that cannot be recaptured, or later accomplished. So, unless the work project cannot possibly be done at a later time, I go to see my daughter run.

Should I go to the political fundraiser at my law partner's home, or spend the night with my family? This one happened to me, and though the partner was not a close friend, nor the political cause an important one to me, I still went. My children were at that time maybe thirteen and ten. Another law partner friend made fun of me for weeks about how "of course you should go to the political event, since your children will never grow up but will be there for you to enjoy endlessly for the rest of your life." I have also heard the adage that few people die wishing they had worked more at the office and seen their family less.

Some decisions deal more with what will produce the best mental state to get all the tasks completed. You may be faced with five projects in a day: one long, arduous project that must be done, and four simpler, less-taxing projects that will not take long individually but will, as a whole, take time to complete. Some people will feel that they cannot have peace of mind until the big project is complete, so they should do it first. Others will say that the feeling of accomplishment in doing the four smaller projects first will put them at ease and make the larger project easier to attack. Stated differently, do you feel better slugging it out to do the large project first, or first completing four projects on the list?

Again, what should be first? Some important life goals, like fitness, require us to simply declare exercise to be an inviolable part of one's day, much like sleep and eating. Some long-term goals, like writing a lengthy piece, embarking on a do-it-yourself fix-it-up project, or creating a vegetable garden, must also be given certain priorities, depending on the value you place upon them. Otherwise, they are unlikely ever to be done.

One also benefits when one does small things in the most efficient and productive order. I turn on my Keurig coffee maker before I go out to get the papers in the morning, so it will be ready to make coffee by the time I return. If I have errands involving four stops in the car, which route will cover all the bases and be the fastest, most efficient, or most aesthetically pleasing? It is particularly pleasing and wise, I believe, to make a list of long-term goals you wish to accomplish, whether it's for travel, preserving mementos, historical sights to visit, trips to see friends, or athletic events you wish to experience. These goals may be given a "first" priority, since they often demand significant planning or work.

Don't Worry About Things You Cannot Alter

Everyone, quite understandably, worries about what will happen in their lives. But we can be far more peaceful by restricting our worries to things we can impact or resolve by our actions. When flying, I literally never worry about dangers, since nothing I can do can alter whatever will happen. I have a friend who is a worrywart who was once described as such a worrier that every day he woke up worried about whether the force of gravity would continue to exist and keep us on earth. Once the test has been submitted, you can't change it, so don't worry about it.

You Are Never a Prophet in Your Own Land

History is replete with stories of persons from distant lands who became prophets, leaders, or beloved and trusted persons. It seems we discount those around us, in our little part of the world, but a stranger has the allure of having different and foreign experiences, new values, and a freshness that our neighbors do not have.

In the working world, you see this when consultants come in to share wisdom with employees and managers. Any idea they have is deemed to be wise and of value, even though an employee may have already suggested it. In family situations, you often see one spouse who seems inclined to believe any stranger on the street over his or her spouse.

One Person's Trash Is Another Person's Treasure

Beginning in about 1957, I began to collect baseball and football cards. I once brought my new 1957 football cards with me on a visit to my friend Randy Spiehs (GISH class of 1967) and compared his 1956 cards from the prior year. It quickly became clear that he thought my new cards were far more desirable. So I began to trade him all my new cards for his prior year cards. I never said a word, but kept thinking, "This guy is crazy. His cards are far more valuable, since I can no longer buy them, but mine are still being sold." I rode away on my bike thinking I had made a great steal. And, as I rode away, I remember overhearing Randy say to his brother Dale, "You won't believe what that dumb Monk did."

Never a Horse That Can't Be Rode and Never a Cowboy That Can't Be "Throwed"

This rodeo metaphor is just a lesson in humility. However adept one might be at a certain event or practice, there is always someone who is better. In *Hamlet* Shakespeare expressed a somewhat similar thought:

Let Hercules himself do what he may,
The cat will meow and dog will have his day."

Even the legendary Hercules is not all powerful.

Homespun Maine Wisdom

My good friends the Fralichs, from Maine, have the classic Maine approach to life that involves wise husbandry of resources. Waste not, want not. I will not expound upon this further, but will just repeat a little saying they taught me:

Buy it new, wear it out.
Make it last, do without.

A Spartan lesson in today's extravagant world, but a wise one, I think. Another great Maine saying they taught me about Maine's weather is "Nine months of winter, and three months of mighty tough sledding."

Time

"Time is the reef upon which most of our dreams eventually crash." I have never forgotten this chilling line after first hearing it. The message, if nothing else, is an incentive to begin to focus more assiduously on achieving our fondest dreams.

Self-Praise Is No Praise

Long ago I saw Groucho Marx on the late-night *Dick Cavett Show*. He was asked a question about his accomplishments and deferred, saying, "Self-praise is no praise, so let's talk about something scandalous or dirty."

A friend of mine from my days at Harvard once told me that he never volunteers that he went to Harvard, since it always has more power if it comes up on its own. Another friend, Marty Kaplan, who has degrees from Harvard (BA), Oxford (master's), and Stanford (PhD), put on his Facebook page, under education, the single entry, "Union High School, Union, New Jersey." The less you brag about your achievements, the more they will be respected.

Always Quickly Tell Friends When You Learn Good News About Them

I have a friend, Bill Creim, in my baseball fantasy league who is a master at sharing good news. The minute he learns one of my players did quite well, he emails, texts, or calls. This practice not only conveys good news, but also associates him with the good news. If he learns of bad news for my team, or otherwise in life, he is silent. He makes his friends feel happy and becomes enmeshed with that happiness. We all know, of course, that one person who is dying to tell you bad news, just so he can see how much it hurts and how you react. These people tend to say they of course did not want to be the one to share the bad news, but they knew you would want to know. Liars!

March 2019

Poetry in Motion

When my good friend and fellow scribe George Ayoub first spoke with me about writing for the GIPS alumni newsletter, he mentioned a vision that included some fiction, some reminiscences, and some poetry. In this piece I want to discuss some poetry that I love.

In high school, and even college, until I studied the Romantic poets, I was much more a fan of prose than poetry. Poetry sometimes seemed artificial and pretentious to me. And indeed, sometimes it still does. But after four years of studying English literature, I completely came around. The best poetry not only has pleasing meter, cadence, and often rhyme, but also wonderful thoughts, expressed with grace and charm. In this piece, I quote two poems and share some of the reasons I love them. Since I believe the meter, or cadence, of a poem is integral to a good poem, I encourage the reader to read the poems below out loud, or at least quietly to yourself.

Since the Distant Mirror looks deep into the past, I begin with poetry from William Shakespeare. The following is from his 1610 play *Cymbeline*, and it reflects upon death.

Fear no more the heat o' the sun

Fear no more the heat o' the sun,
Nor the furious winter's rages;
Thou thy worldly task hast done,
Home art gone, and ta'en thy wages:
Golden lads and girls all must,
As chimney-sweepers, come to dust.

Fear no more the frown o' the great;
Thou art past the tyrant's stroke;
Care no more to clothe and eat;
To thee the reed is as the oak:
The scepter, learning, physic, must
All follow this, and come to dust.

Fear no more the lightning flash,
Nor the all-dreaded thunder stone;
Fear not slander, censure rash;
Thou hast finished joy and moan:
All lovers young, all lovers must
Consign to thee, and come to dust.

No exorciser harm thee!
Nor no witchcraft charm thee!
Ghost unlaid forbear thee!
Nothing ill come near thee!

Quiet consummation have;
And renownèd be thy grave!

—WILLIAM SHAKESPEARE, *Cymbeline*, act 4, scene 2

These beautiful, yet very sobering, lines remind us that all the troubles of life are behind us when we die. Death, for all its gruesome reality, does free us from all our worldly cares. Several things are interesting in this poem. Shakespeare does not promise or discuss an afterlife or what exists when life is over. Indeed, he notes only the cold reality of coming "to dust."

But the unstated thought is that most of us would choose life over death even with the tyrant's stroke, the lightning flash, and the slander and censure rash, since with them also come the joys and pleasures of life. Maybe when living, we should be willing to better tolerate the vicissitudes of life, given the joys that accompany them.

Next is a wonderful poem by Emily Dickinson. It talks about success and who prizes it most.

Success is counted sweetest

Success is counted sweetest
By those who ne'er succeed.
To comprehend a nectar
Requires sorest need.

Not one of all the purple Host
Who took the Flag today
Can tell the definition
So clear of victory

As he defeated—dying—
On whose forbidden ear

The distant strains of triumph
Burst agonized and clear!

—Emily Dickinson (1859)

    Our successes are at times taken for granted, and Dickinson posits that success is most valued by those who fail to succeed. The dramatic vision of the soldier "defeated—dying" reflects that he, more than anyone, knows the true value of the victory in battle. The wonderful phrase "To comprehend a nectar requires sorest need" also implies that only with great need of food, and perhaps with little experience with a "nectar," can one comprehend its value.

    As a final note on Dickinson, I learned long ago that this poem, and indeed most of her poems, can be sung to the tune of "The Yellow Rose of Texas." If you don't know the song, look it up on YouTube, and you will find that the words of this poem fit perfectly.

    Lastly, while many of us love music and can sing the words of our favorite songs, we may lose sight of the fact that this is poetry too. While often less formal, the message can still be inspiring and uplifting.

    So, fear not the poem that may come in your path. Indeed, go hog wild and read some Dickinson, some Frost, some Whitman. You might even find you like it.

May 2019

Grade School Crime and Punishment

The Spitball Incident:

*April 1960, Howard School, Grand Island,
Mrs. Severson's Fifth and Sixth Combination Room*

On this April day, the beloved Mrs. Severson was not present, and an older lady was filling in as a substitute. The class immediately sensed this substitute was not a disciplinarian. Her newness and passive approach would provide chances for some fun. A couple of the more daring miscreants in the class began to throw spitballs, formed by taking some paper in your mouth and wetting it into a ball. My recollection is that Steve Schroeder and Mike Parmley were the ringleaders. They, of course, were not new to trouble. Earlier in the year, the class had planned a surprise "fruit roll" for Mrs. Severson, an event where apples, grapefruit, and oranges would be rolled to the front of the class as an act of kindness and source of gifts for the teacher. The whole class was in on the surprise, and all the students were excited to please the teacher. But of course, Steve Schroeder had to push it too far, and he threw, rather than rolled, a large watermelon, which split open, causing a huge mess near the teacher's desk. This resulted in a very angry Mrs. Severson and likely put a permanent end to the "fruit roll" tradition.

But on this day, it was spitballs. At first, Schroeder and Parmley threw the spitballs only when the substitute teacher's back was turned. But when nothing happened, they began to throw them in more risky situations. Soon, most of the class joined in, including the notorious "good boy," yours truly, Mike Monk. While a few upstanding girls made faces and did not participate, virtually all of the boys began throwing them, and a good number of girls too. It was exciting and fun. I sensed, however, that the teacher had to have noticed this uprising, though she did not let on. I also sensed we were all on thin ice.

When the substitute teacher left the classroom for a moment, all heck broke loose, and soon most of the students were up out of their seats, running around and pummeling classmates with spitballs. Mike Parmley was shouting and egging others on. One student went to the chalkboard and wrote, "Shut Up, Parmley." Just then, the teacher returned to the room. She obviously then saw the full extent of the uprising, and order was soon returned to the classroom. The teacher then proceeded, in front of the entire class, to investigate the matter. Who started it? Which students were involved? Did anyone try to stop it?

Soon informants were rising up and ratting out the ringleaders and those most involved. It was amazing how willing fifth and sixth graders were to throw others under the bus. The Madame Defarges of the grade school set were happy to convict. Maybe because they were sincerely annoyed by the commotion, maybe to get even with an adversary, or maybe to hope for lenient treatment themselves. Or, God forbid, maybe they were just good citizens. The investigation also involved questions about who did not participate. Someone said Gloria Callahan (who later became a teacher herself) didn't throw any spitballs, and someone else said Peggy Burger also did not throw any spitballs. Other girls, too, were identified as not being involved in the melee. Then it evolved to students saying that certain people participated but didn't throw many, just a few, and so forth. While I had thrown my share, I hoped someone would say that while Mike threw some, he was not as bad as the leaders. And near the end of the uprising, I did make a soft suggestion that we might cool it. But no such support emerged for me. So the innocent and the guilty were identified, with surprising gradations of guilt being assessed.

The punishment, as I vaguely recall, was somewhat minor. I think the worst transgressors were required to clean the chalkboards and erasers for a week or so, or miss recess, or take on some similarly minimal duty. While it may have happened, I do not recall any parents being contacted or any more severe punishment. The real punishment was being outed in public. It was embarrassing, and everyone observed it. And it left a sense of being judged by one's peers. It certainly gave me the awareness that transgressions will likely be discovered, and it was not worth the thrill to get caught and publicly embarrassed. The sense that the entire class was involved in the process left no room for anyone to complain about how anyone was treated.

But now let the Distant Mirror move forward thirty-nine years, to California.

The Pokémon Incident:

April 1999, the Carden School of Santa Monica, California, Ms. Monk's Second-Grade Class and Ms. Amato's Third-Grade Class

In 1999, my wife was the owner and director of a small private K-through-six grade school in Santa Monica. That same year, prior to going to law school, my daughter, Susannah, taught second grade at the school. There were many good students in the second-grade class, including two Japanese American boys who were very bright and lots of fun. I was always fond of them for two reasons. Once Susannah overheard them talking and one of them asked the other, "If you could marry any teacher, which one would you marry?" and the answer was "Ms. Monk." Also, once when Ms. Monk told them a spelling quiz was over, time was up, and they had to stop writing, one of these boys kept on writing. Pursuant to the rules, his quiz paper was collected before he could finish. He was furious, and Ms. Monk later found a mock report card he prepared with all students getting straight *A*s and Ms. Monk getting a *Z*.

In April of that year, the Pokémon fad was in full swing. One of the Japanese American boys' father took a trip to Japan and brought back Pokémon pencils and erasers as presents for him and for all of his second-grade classmates. These were prized possessions. Shortly after the pencils were given out, during a second-grade recess, the third-grade class used the second-grade room. At some point, a third-grade boy surreptitiously took most of the pencils from the second-grade students' desks. When the second graders returned, they were distraught to find their prized possessions gone.

But soon enough, some other third-grade pupils saw the pencils and erasers and ratted out the boy who had taken them. Once again, much like the spitball event at Howard School, an open and immediate investigation took place. While I do not recall the gory details, I do recall that the boy who stole the pencils and erasers was questioned by the third-grade teacher, Ms. Amato, in front of his class. The accusers confirmed finding the loot in his desk, and he eventually confessed to the crime. The second graders not only had their pencils and erasers returned, but they learned that the thief was confronted, convicted, and outed in person. Once again, I do not recall the precise punishment imposed, but I again think that the most painful punishment was the open forum in which his deeds were confirmed and at which he eventually confessed. These second and third graders, too, had a sense that the community had acted in concert, with nothing behind closed doors, and that justice had been served.

And as with the spitball investigation, I do not recall any adverse comments by parents. The teachers were trusted and not questioned.

The 2019 Grade School Crime and Punishment

I have rarely been in a grade school classroom in the past twenty years, and then only to meet my grandchildren's teachers on the first day of school. But I wonder how grade school crimes like spitballs and stealing pencils would be treated today. I strongly suspect that the Spanish Inquisition style used in the 1960 spitball crisis and the 1999 Pokémon crisis would not be used or welcomed today.

I can just hear today's parents ranting that their child had been singled out, was embarrassed, and now needed counseling and therapy. They would contend that the teacher violated the student's privacy and abused the child with open accusations and punishment. I can see lawyers writing sternly worded letters and threatening lawsuits. I can see letters to the local newspaper decrying the brutal and insensitive treatment and suggesting the ouster of teachers and the principal. I can see the parents indeed blaming their child's behavior on the teacher, for some transgression or mistake the teacher had made, which of course was the direct cause of the poor child's misbehavior.

I speculate that today the investigation would likely be done privately, and the results perhaps not even conveyed to the other students, to protect the accused student's "privacy."

Which is the better approach? I do not pretend to know, and I am not a trained educator. And I know that such matters are clearly more complex today. But I think there is some value in the old approach. It creates the sense among the students that the matter was taken seriously and immediately addressed. It has the value and credibility of being a process in which everyone was involved. It was transparent. And for me at least, the public shaming made me think long and hard about any future misbehavior.

But I do understand that schools must act in accordance with the times. And I sense the times now, even in the relative haven of an excellent Midwestern grade school, would not permit a public examination of the crime and the punishment. I would be delighted to hear from the GIPS nation as to how such matters are handled today, and thoughts on how they should be handled.

July 2019

Recollections of Mike Parmley, Class of 1967

On May 10, 2019, my 1967 GISH classmate Mike Parmley passed away. On the day this newsletter comes out, July 15, 2019, he would have been seventy years old. He was an extraordinary fellow and my close friend since second grade in 1956 in Miss Langdon's class at Howard School. From 1975 until the late 1990s, when he retired to Nebraska, Parm was the clown prince and the charismatic center of a very close group of friends in California. The group included fellow 1967 classmates Bob Johnsen, Jerry Stroud, and myself, plus Bob's wife, Donna (Plattsmouth), Jack Oldham, GIHS class of 1965, Tom Housel (from Lexington), J. D. Graninetti (from Omaha), and Nancy Sanstedt (from Omaha). Following are two stories I wrote some time ago about Parm, drawn closely from his reports of the events at the time.

November 22, 1988—Ninth and Pine Street, Grand Island

Little Davie Parmley, Mike Parmley's six-year-old nephew, was twitching with excitement. His uncle Mike from California was visiting Nebraska. Uncle Mike was that rare grown-up who seemed to think like a kid would think. Uncle Mike's idea of fun was usually close to his nephews' and nieces' views of fun, and he consistently let them do things their parents would never approve.

Uncle Mike had just returned from hunting, and as he walked in the house, the smell of mud, pheasants, and the outdoors filled the room. Davie followed devotedly as Parm took one particularly bloody pheasant and quietly sought out his nephew Bobby, who was watching cartoons on television in the den.

"Oh, honey," said Ellen, Parm's mother, who smiled involuntarily as she saw her son holding a battered bird by its legs and heading toward the den. "Don't frighten the children." Parm drew his free hand to his mouth to quiet his mother and slipped up quickly behind Bobby, with nephew Davie following close on his heels.

Parm jumped in front of Bobby and dangled the dead bird in front of him, loudly shouting, "Whoa! . . . There's a big one, it's flying low and somebody is going to shoot it. . . . *Bamm! Bamm!* . . . It's been hit! Look out!"

Parm then flung the bird in Bobby's lap. As with many of Parm's antics with his nephews, nieces, and his buddy Mucker's kids, his audacity often initially brought them to tears, particularly in the younger years. They learned quickly, however, that Uncle Mike's exploits were usually harmless. Not always, but usually.

Here the damage was moderate. Bobby wasn't crying, and only a little bit of the blood from the bird had stained Bobby's shirt and the couch.

Bobby at first jumped and shrank back in fear. Once he realized that the bird was dead, however, he lost his fear and tossed the bird back at Parm. His aim, though, was foul. The bird struck the coffee table, knocking off the ashtray and the paper turkey decoration anticipating the upcoming Thanksgiving holiday.

"Now boys," said Ellen, "see what you've done." Ellen's smile remained, though she tried to appear stern.

"Now look what you've done," said Parm to Bobby. "Let's clean this up for your grandmother." Parm, Bobby, and Davie all began to clean up the mess, with Bobby whispering to Parm, "You started it, Uncle Mike."

"Now, let's not start pointing fingers," said Parm, who had in the previous instant been pointing the finger at Bobby.

Later That Day . . .

"Uncle Mike," said Davie, "will you take out your eye for us again?"

"Now, Davie, you know I can't do that too often because it's not good for my eye."

"But, Uncle Mike, you haven't done it once yet this trip."

"Well, okay—but I want everybody to be really careful, because it's very dangerous if you drop it. Let me go to the bathroom first— you get all the gang in the basement, make sure it's totally dark, and I'll be right down. Now don't say a word to your grandmother."

Davie, Bobby, and little Mikey, Parm's three-year-old nephew, headed noisily to the basement, shouting to each other. "We've got to be careful!" "It's so slippery!" "Don't tell Grandma Ellen!"

Parm went to the refrigerator and selected three green grapes. As he headed to the bathroom on the main floor, he could hear his nephews giggling and laughing below in the basement. He went into the bathroom, carefully chose the grape closest in size to his eye, and slowly peeled the grape until all the skin was gone. Then Parm accidentally dropped the fleshy grape. "Oh crap," he whispered to himself. He picked up the peeled grape and then washed it off in the sink, leaving it a little slick and mushy. He then placed the grape in his shirt pocket and went down the wooden stairs to the darkened basement. He quietly slipped into what was his old bedroom when he lived at home as a boy.

He saw the children in the dark, closed the door, and whispered softly, "Shuuuuush. Now young folks, step back, and your uncle Mike will take out his eye, but here are the rules: Number one, we got to keep it totally dark—let's close this shade even lower—or my eye will be damaged; number two, whatever you do, don't drop it, or your uncle Mike could lose his sight in that eye, especially if we step on it."

"Uncle Mike, does it hurt when you take it out?" asked Mikey.

"Well, it does hurt a little bit, but if you handle it real carefully, it's not too bad," said Parm, nodding slowly. The room was now dark enough that it was difficult to see his nephews. He reached into his pocket for the grape and cried out, "Oooooh . . . aaaaaah . . . there . . . okay."

"Is it out, Uncle Mike?"

"Ah! Yes, I've got it out. Now here, Davie, be as careful as you can possibly be."

Davie gently cradled the grape in his grimy hand with an eerie feeling churning in his stomach at the thought of actually holding his uncle Mike's eye in his hands. "It's so slippery, Uncle Mike, I'm afraid I'll drop it."

"Well, be careful, for Christ's sake," said Parm, feigning anger at Davie's actions.

Next Bobby held the grape, and he silently dug his fingernail into the grape, looked up at where he thought his uncle Mike was, and neither felt, nor heard, any indication of pain from his uncle.

"My turn," said little Mikey, and he grabbed at Bobby's hand, trying to find the eye. Bobby handed Mikey the eye, and as he did, he felt Mikey pinch the eye.

"Mikey's pinching your eye, Uncle Mike."

"Hey, son, what are you doing with my eye! Oooooh, ouch, stop it!"

Mikey couldn't understand why Uncle Mike cried out in pain at times when he wasn't pinching the eye. Maybe it still hurts later even after I pinch it, he thought.

Parm then took the grimy grape from Mikey, popped it into his mouth, took one chew, and swallowed it, pronouncing, "Whew, I think I have it back in safely. I can see with both eyes now."

Later during Parm's trip, the nephews wanted to have him take out the eye again, but he staunchly refused. "No, I can't take that chance more than once during a trip to Husker land." But he did show them how he could take his index finger off, oh so briefly, and how he could stick his finger in his ear, thrust it through his head, and poke the opposite cheek from the inside of his mouth.

September 2019

About Time

Today, as we peer into the Distant Mirror, we observe my seventh-grade science class at Walnut, in 1962. On this day our teacher showed the class a wonderful Bell Telephone educational film called *About Time*. I was amused by the title, which was both a simple description of the subject and yet invoked the common phrase that it is "about time" something was done. And I loved the film, which examined the concept of time, including Einstein's theory of relativity, which to this day is a hard one for me to grasp.

In the film, a cartoon displayed how a brother took a spaceship to a distant planet and returned many years later. But when he returned, his twin brother had aged, now looking far older than he. But the space traveler looked not much older than when he had departed. The lesson was that traveling away from the gravity of Earth alters the passage of time. Experiments have indeed shown that a watch on a high mountain (farther from Earth's gravity) will run ever so slightly more slowly than one at sea level. One supposedly simple explanation of Einstein's theory says, "All motion must be defined relative to a frame of reference, since space and time are relative, rather than absolute concepts." Say what? Isn't ten minutes always ten minutes?

More recently I read the Stephen Hawking book entitled *Brief Answers to the Big Questions*. It expresses the theory that time began only with the Big Bang and that there was no time prior thereto. Once again, I am stupefied. What happened two hours before the Big Bang? Does not time go back endlessly prior to any event and will it not continue without end after any given event?

This concept reminds me of the Meat Loaf song "Paradise by the Dashboard Light." The song describes a man trying to seduce his girlfriend in the car, by the dashboard light. She will relent only if he "promises to love her till the end of time." So he promises to love her till the end of time. But by the end of the song, he regrets the decision and says, "So now I'm praying for the end of time to hurry up and arrive, 'cause if I have to spend another minute with you, I don't think that I can really survive."

There are also countless aphorisms about time. Some I have heard forever, but for which I do not know the source:

"Time waits for no one."

"Time races for the man who will be taken to the gallows to be hung in one hour."

"Time crawls for the youth awaiting the arrival of his lover."

"Time marches on!"

Others come from songs or literature:

"To every thing there is a season, and a time to every purpose under the heaven."

—Ecclesiastes 3:1

"Do not squander time. That is the stuff life is made of."
 —from a clock in the classic movie *Gone with the Wind*

"Yeah, Beavis, I don't have time for a yeast infection either."
 —from the TV show *Beavis and Butt-Head*

"Time is very slow for those who wait. Very fast for those who are scared. Very long for those who lament. Very short for those who celebrate. But for those who love, time is eternal."
 —Henry van Dyke

"Come what come may, / Time and the hour runs through the roughest day."
 —Shakespeare, *Macbeth*, act 1, scene 3

Time also appears to pass at different rates at different ages. When you are six years old, it seems to take forever to get to seven. So my grandson, Leo, like many at that age, says he is six and a half years old. When you are sixty, however, you seem to turn seventy in the wink of an eye. I speak from experience on this one. The perception of time in later years is like a coin that is circling round and round on its edge, at first slowly and then increasingly more rapidly, until it comes to an abrupt stop.

As we age, the decreasing and uncertain amount of time left to live becomes more precious. We now more clearly realize it must be used most wisely. To the extent you are able, you start to avoid any activity that does not "spark joy." You try to fill your life with those activities that bring you pleasure or achieve lifelong goals. You create a bucket list. I joke with family and friends, "If you have a cranberry muffin and a blueberry muffin in the refrigerator, and you prefer the cranberry, eat it first." You may never get to the other one.

I was on the floor laughing recently after my grandson, Leo, asked in total seriousness, "Grandpa, when your two dogs die, will you and Grandma get new dogs . . . if you are still alive?"

A few years back, I heard an unflinchingly brutal phrase, which

I mentioned before: "Time is the reef upon which most of our dreams eventually crash."

This chilling thought encourages me to do the things I really want to do now, not "when I get around to it."

"And you, of tender years," as Crosby, Stills, Nash & Young sang, can also benefit from this approach. You never know how long Grandma Betsy will be here. If you love her, tell her so now. You never know what tomorrow will hold. In short, follow your bliss. This includes not only your passions, but good deeds, rest, reflection, exercise, health, and attacking those adventures or projects that have significant meaning to you.

About twenty years ago or so, my close friend and 1967 GIHS classmate Bob Johnsen went to the Kentucky Derby. When he returned, I asked him what motivated the trip. He said he loved horse racing, and the Kentucky Derby was the pinnacle of the sport. He further elaborated that he did not want people at his funeral saying, "Yes, Bob had a wonderful life, but, you know, he never made it to the Kentucky Derby." Four years ago, Bob passed away at the young age of sixty-six. I spoke at his funeral and reminded everyone that Bob had indeed made it to the Kentucky Derby.

Of course, during much of our lifetime, we have work, family, and other unavoidable obligations that require and demand our time and attention. Life cannot be simply a pursuit of joyous or meaningful activities. But when you have time that you can decide how to use, at any age, use it wisely. Embrace your passions, plan for the future, treasure your friends and loved ones, appreciate the beauty all around you, and seek happiness. The last thing Lydia Severson, my fifth-grade teacher at Howard, said on the final day of fifth grade, just before we left the classroom, was, "Don't take things too seriously. Life is just a bowl of cherries."

Well, I have spent enough time on this piece. It is about time I wrapped it up. Until next time!

November 2019

The Magic of Sports Uniforms

As we peer into the Distant Mirror today, we travel back sixty-five years to 1954 in Amherst, Nebraska, a town of maybe five hundred people, just northwest of Kearney. We see the Amherst High School football team in a Friday night game against neighboring Riverdale. It was the first football game I ever saw. These big high school kids were tackling each other, throwing passes, and running with the football, and it was magic. I was five years old, and I was hooked. I particularly recall the red and silver uniforms the Amherst team wore, which I thought were beautiful. I remember getting a silver and red jacket that I prized. Later that year, we moved to the big city, Grand Island.

As I grew and my fascination with sports grew with me, I became enamored of all the sports uniforms I saw. Like many young fans, for me the uniforms were part of the glamour and attraction of sports. I mostly examined uniforms from the baseball and football cards I collected, since there was then only a single baseball game of the week on television on Saturday, and one game a week of pro football, on Sunday.

Along with my buddies George Ayoub and Bob McFarland and my cousin Randy Garroutte, I worshipped the New York Yankees and their classic pinstripe uniforms with the iconic hat with the *N* overlaying the *Y*. I thought that was the coolest thing ever. We all loved Mickey Mantle, and any kid in Little League who got to have number 7 was truly blessed. Generally the coach's son got number 7; in my case, that was my friend Steve Burton. This was particularly great, since we both were on the "Yanks." My favorite baseball card ever is the Topps 1957 card with Mickey Mantle and Yogi Berra. Their hats were dark blue with the overlapping *NY*. The brim was virtually straight, not curved and bent into an arc, as later became the fad. For the rest of my life I have tried to make my baseball hats look the same way.

Football uniforms were cool, too, with the helmets, colored piping, and numerals. I particularly liked the horseshoe on the helmet of the Colts. When I was first a fan, there were no face guards, and then they came out with a single bar across the face to protect the player, and I thought that was pretty neat. I also loved the hockey uniforms. A big jersey with shoulder pads underneath, then these wonderful baggy shorts, and beneath them tights and other pads. Thank goodness they have not changed much.

It was, therefore, a magic day when I got my first Little League uniform and the matching hat. Later the same joy was there when I donned the Walnut and, later, Senior High football, basketball, and track uniforms.

I have come to believe that the uniforms teams wore when I first started watching sports in the 1950s are still the coolest, and that any change is a radical departure from what uniforms should be. This, I think, is the square one from which many of us operate.

In the 1950s, home baseball teams wore white with the nickname on the jersey (Red Sox, Pirates, Phillies, etc.). The visiting teams wore gray with the name of the city on the jersey (Cleveland, Chicago, etc.). A couple teams had these gorgeous pictures, notably the Cardinals, with a cardinal sitting on each end of a baseball bat. There was also the wonderful Tiger uniform with the classy Old English *D* on the front.

Pants came down just below the knee, with the socks showing. There was a colored sock with high stirrups and beneath it, a white "sanitary" sock. This was because in the early years of baseball, teams were often called by the color of their socks, i.e., the Boston Red Sox, the Chicago White Sox, and others. But the dye of the colored socks had an ingredient such that if a player was spiked (Ty Cobb and other earlier players often tried to spike infielders), the dye would get in the open wound and cause infections. This led to the change where the colored sock would have stirrups, with a white "sanitary" sock underneath. This look was the standard in the 1950s when I first began to follow baseball, and I loved it. The longer the stirrups, the better.

Over the years, I saw baseball uniforms slowly change. I watched in the 1970s as the Oakland A's wore these gaudy bright yellow and green uniforms. I kind of liked them, but they seemed insufficiently dignified. Later, I saw teams with crazy new approaches. The White Sox one year wore shorts instead of pants, leaving bare skin showing above the socks. An outrage! This didn't last long, since sliding was painful with the bare skin exposed. I also saw the teams begin to change from the classic white for the home team and gray for the visitors. Teams were wearing dark-colored tops with white pants, sometimes dark tops and pants. The old Houston Astros had these psychedelic uniforms mixing shades of orange, yellow, and blue and looking frightful to my eye.

And finally, about twenty or so years ago, came the abomination of baseball players wearing pants so long, they looked like pajama bottoms that were too big. They completely covered the socks below, slumping down over the spikes, looking pathetic and ridiculous. This trend continues to this day, but I have good news. More and more, I see the players wearing a shorter pant that actually shows the socks, which I find much more aesthetically pleasing.

In football, the basic structure of the uniforms has not changed, but oh, the bright and glossy colors! I remember the first Nebraska uniforms, with the scarlet jerseys and cream pants and numerals with a curved, swirling look, not the block numbers of today. The rage today is the neon glow look on both uniforms and helmets. The Oregon Ducks started this, I think, with a variety of loud and glossy green and yellow uniforms. Also, teams now will don a variety of uniforms both at home and on the road. I just about threw up when I saw the Huskers in all-red uniforms for the first time. I have to admit, however, that in general the new football uniforms, glossy helmets and all, look pretty good to me.

The major change in basketball uniforms has been the length of the shorts. Forever, basketball players wore a tank top to allow full movement and shorts that were indeed short. This changed with the Fab Five Michigan team of the 1990s. They started wearing shorts that were much longer, just a few inches above the knee. The trend continued to where shorts became longer and longer. Eventually, some shorts fell beneath the knee. This seemed laughable to me, but with time, a longer short has come to seem normal. As I now watch tapes of the old Magic Johnson–Larry Bird showdowns, the shorts look embarrassingly short, like "tighty-whities" underwear!

I can sum up my general feelings by saying that whenever teams now wear "throwback" jerseys, they look goofy and old, but I usually like them better than the current uniforms.

My list of favorite classic uniforms—stylish, tasteful, and bold—includes:

1. New York Yankee pinstripes with the overlapping *NY* on the jersey.
2. The Chicago Blackhawk hockey jersey with the beautiful drawing of a proud Native American.
3. The Green Bay Packer yellow and green uniform, with the iconic *G*, ensconced in a circle, on the helmet.
4. The Nebraska football away uniform with the white jersey and red pants.
5. The Princeton University football uniform from the 1950s with orange circular piping on sleeves of a black jersey.
6. The St. Louis Cardinal uniform with the two red birds perched on the baseball bat.
7. The Detroit Red Wing snappy white hockey jersey with the classic wing on the front.

I close with a quick comment about sporting crowds. With Leo, my sports crazy grandson, I go to lots of games. In the past two years, we have gone together to college and professional soccer, basketball, football, hockey, baseball, and volleyball games. The trend that bothers me greatly is that at many contests, mostly soccer and football games, certain parts of the crowd have come to believe they must stand for most of the game. For those like me who prefer to sit, this is a major pain in the whatever. If we all sit, we all see.

One can be a completely avid fan without standing for the whole game. I think this trend started with the maniacal Duke basketball students who feel compelled to jump up and down the entire freaking game. This standing phenomenon has also spread to concerts. I now desperately troll StubHub for seats in a front row of a section or balcony or other location where I can sit on my bottom and enjoy the game or concert.

January 2020

Christmas Memories

Today, the Distant Mirror looks back to Christmas memories from the 1950s. In the recent holiday season, I thought back to some particularly joyous memories at Howard School in the 1950s. Each Christmas season, on several occasions, the entire school would convene in the foyer. Sitting with classmates on the floor, with crossed legs then known as "Indian style," we would sing Christmas carols. For me, this was a transcendent joy. I loved the carols for the kindness, togetherness, and joy they celebrated. I liked the religious songs as well as the Santa, Rudolph, and Frosty songs, but just singing together as a school was magnificent.

For the last thirty-five years, we have attended the holiday party at the home of our friends Larry and Sally Yeatman in Santa Monica, California. One of our friends, Jim Perkins, is an excellent pianist and can play virtually all the carols, so the party ends with all of us singing as a group. It remains one of the highlights of my year. I simply love caroling, but the practice of groups of people going door-to-door caroling is not nearly as common as in the 1950s. I hope we do not completely lose this glorious tradition.

Top Five Favorite Christmas Carols and Holiday Songs:

1. "Good King Wenceslas"
2. "O Holy Night" (my mother's favorite)
3. "Silent Night"
4. "O Come, All Ye Faithful"
5. Adam Sandler's "Hanukkah Song"

"Good King Wenceslas" was not among my top carols growing up, but it has now become my favorite Christmas song. The lyrics are poetic and beautiful. They don't directly address religion, but rather tell the simple story of a monarch and his page. They see a poor man gathering winter fuel though "the snow lay round about, deep and crisp and even." Together the king and the page trod through bitter cold to bring the peasant flesh and wine and pine logs. The last lines are:

Therefore, Christian men, be sure,
Wealth or rank possessing,
Ye who now will bless the poor,
Shall yourselves find blessing.

Is that not a wonderful holiday sentiment?

"O Holy Night" is a beautiful song also, peaceful and comforting. "Silent Night" and "O Come, All Ye Faithful" are similar. I am a huge fan of Adam Sandler's "Hanukkah Song." While a bit racy and very modern, it celebrates the Jewish tradition and many Jewish luminaries with humor and affection.

Top Silly Words to Holiday and Patriotic Songs

1. *Jingle bells, Batman smells, Robin laid an egg,*
The Batmobile lost a wheel and the Joker got away.

2. *We three kings of Orient are,*
Tried to smoke a rubber cigar.
It was loaded, it exploded,
The noise was heard near and far.

3. *God bless my underwear,*
They are my only pair.
Stand beside them and guide them
Through the rips, through the holes, through the tears,
From the washer, to the dryer, to the clothesline in the air,
God bless my underwear, my only pair

Best Punk Version of Religious Christmas Carols

Bad Religion's *Christmas Songs* album

This CD is a real gem. Using punk rock guitars and rapid drumming, the band Bad Religion sings the most prominent religious carols in an upbeat, creative manner. And it works! I highly recommend this album.

Favorite Christmas and Holiday Movies

As a lifelong film buff and movie follower, I am a real softie for a great Christmas movie. My favorites are:

1. *A Christmas Carol* – 1951 movie with Alastair Sim as Scrooge
2. *It's a Wonderful Life* – 1946 movie with James Stewart and Donna Reed
3. *The Bishop's Wife* – 1947 movie with Cary Grant, Loretta

Young, and David Niven
4. *Scrooged* – 1988 movie with Bill Murray
5. *Elf* – 2003 movie with Will Ferrell, James Caan, and Zooey Deschanel
6. *A Christmas Story* – 1983 movie featuring Ralphie trying to get the Red Ryder BB gun

By far the most famous and ubiquitous is *A Christmas Carol*, with dozens of movies based on the Charles Dickens classic novella. Some say this book was the true beginning of celebrating Christmas as we know it. Well known to all, I will just address my favorite part, which is when Scrooge finally sees the light and finds new joy in being generous. The scene where he shouts to a lad on the street to go buy the big goose down the block for the Cratchit family is wonderful. The technique of using the ghost of Marley, and subsequently the ghosts of Christmas Past, Christmas Present, and Christmas Future, is brilliant and has been used by many later films.

In December of 1973, in my second year of law school, just before the holiday break, I turned on my little black-and-white TV and started watching a movie where some angels were deciding which guardian angel should go down to earth and help George Bailey. I had never seen or heard of the movie but quickly became entranced and watched the whole thing. *It's a Wonderful Life* came into my life. I loved it. Only later did the movie become a regular holiday tradition and become so well known. For decades my family never failed to watch it on Christmas Eve. It is indeed an extraordinary movie, showing the huge impact a single human can have on so many people. The technique of having a guardian angel show George Bailey what the world would be like without him is not all that different from Scrooge being shown the Christmas Past, Present, and Future. I have probably seen this movie fifty times, more than once on the big screen here in Santa Monica at the Aero Theatre, run now by the American Cinematheque, but I still always get teary at the end when Harry Bailey toasts his brother George as "the richest man in town."

The original *Bishop's Wife* is a wonderful classic film that is not so well known. It also uses the technique of a guardian angel (here Cary Grant) who comes down to help the bishop, David Niven, with his problems. The angel charms everyone and eventually helps the bishop find the right path to happiness. Once the angel leaves, no one remembers him.

Scrooged closely follows the plot of *A Christmas Carol*, with the obnoxious television mogul Bill Murray visited by hilarious Ghosts of Christmas Past, Present, and Future. Much like in his epic *Groundhog Day*, Murray changes from a self-centered jerk to someone who finally acts with the milk of human kindness.

Elf is also a charming little movie, and I think Will Ferrell's best acting job ever. Here Ferrell's father, James Caan, sees the light and gains the Christmas spirit.

Finally, the ever-so-charming *A Christmas Story*, the tale of young Ralphie, who seeks the Red Ryder BB gun, the dad who covets the fishnet-stocking leg lamp he won, and the boy who licks the frozen pipe and gets his tongue stuck. This film also holds up very well. The scene of Christmas dinner at a Chinese restaurant after the turkey is eaten by the neighbor's dogs is a classic.

By the way, this past December, I watched each of these movies again, except for *The Bishop's Wife*, which I missed.

Whatever your faith, or lack thereof, to me these movies and songs celebrate some of the best aspects of human behavior. At the end of *The Bishop's Wife*, the bishop gives a sermon that was written by his guardian angel that ends with these lines:

"Let us ask ourselves what He [Jesus] would wish for most. And then let each put in his share. Loving kindness, warm hearts, and a stretched-out hand of tolerance. All the shining gifts that make peace on earth."

A belated, but vigorous, happy holidays to all!

March 2020

Equal Treatment of Siblings

Each year, for over four decades, my close law school friend John Fowler and I have had a college football bet. We have a draft before the season begins in which we each pick six different college teams. Each week we add up the AP ranking for our top five teams (throwing out the worst team), and the low score wins. The weekly winner gets $20. Also, when one of my teams plays one of his teams, the winner of each "matchup" wins $20. Also, the winner of the final poll at the year's end gets $40. And if either of us picks the national champion, that is also worth $40. Generally one of us will win one or two hundred dollars, but some years we just about break even.

This past August, when John and I were getting ready to have our draft, my sports-loving six-year-old grandson, Leo, whom I have written about previously, wanted to know about the bet. I explained it, and Leo said he wanted to help pick teams. So we examined the preseason rankings, ranked our favorites, and got ready to draft. "Grandpa, you have to get Alabama" was just one of his pieces of advice. I told Leo that I sometimes lost money and sometimes won money, but that if we won money this year, I would share it fifty-fifty with him. He was in! He told me he had already saved up $14, from tooth fairy money and other gifts.

As the season progressed, our teams won virtually every week's $20 prize and also did well in matchups. Luckily, we had picked LSU, Alabama, and Georgia, each of which had good years. Throughout the fall, Leo and I would watch games on Saturday and root for our squads. After each week, I would tell him where we stood. Near the end of the season, we were ahead $260, and we had a chance to win more with LSU in the national championship game. He was getting more and more excited.

When Leo and family were at our house in California for the Christmas break, Leo and I went to my friend Tom Housel's house, where we joined Tom and friends Jon Light and David Bordeaux to watch the LSU–Oklahoma national championship semifinal game. This was also a matchup, since we had LSU and John had Oklahoma. LSU dominated the game. Leo was up high-fiving me and my buddies and dancing after every LSU touchdown. My daughter, Susannah, Leo's mother, and I also took Leo to the Rose Bowl in Pasadena on New Year's Day. We saw one of our teams, Oregon, win a thriller. Leo was pumped up. LSU then went on to win the national championship, and after the dust settled, Leo and I had won $360—$180 for me and $180 for Leo.

I then called Leo, who was back in Minnesota, and we rejoiced in our winnings. But on that call, in the background, I heard Leo's nine-year-old sister, Victoria, and she asked, "What about me, Grandpa?" I explained that Leo had helped me pick teams and had helped me root for them all year long, and that he had been part of the bet. She then replied, "But what about me, Grandpa?" I lamely said that I would do something for her too.

Later, my son-in-law explained to Victoria that "you have to be in it to win it." But this did not satisfy her, and I understood why. Her brother had been given an opportunity that she was not given, and that did not seem fair. But I thought it would send the wrong message to simply give her $180 too.

So I told her, "Victoria, I love you so much, and you are my best girl, so while I will not give you money, I will let you pick out a present or two that you would really like." She thought long and carefully and finally said, "I would really like a harmonica." She then added, "And I would like some 'hair chalk.'" I then learned that "hair chalk" is something fourth-grade girls use to dye their hair weird colors, but it washes right out. So I immediately bought her a nice harmonica and some hair chalk, and she was a happy camper. It had been wise not to suggest ways to make things even, but to let her declare what would do so. And it worked, thank goodness.

By the way, Victoria also has announced that next year, she wants to help pick teams and be part of the bet. Leo then immediately exclaimed, "But she doesn't know anything about football!"

This story barely scratches the surface of the challenge of treating sibling children, or grandchildren, equally. Woe be it to the parent who gives one child the best bedroom, the most time, the sweetest smile, or anything that is viewed as superior by another sibling. When my two children were young, we bought a three-bedroom house with a master bedroom, a large second bedroom, and a much smaller third bedroom. We gave the large bedroom to Susannah, our older daughter, and the lesser bedroom to her younger brother, James, who was just two years old when we bought the house. When they grew older, we eventually got them used cars. Assessing the cars we bought and the small bedroom, our son hinted that he might have been shorted somehow in all this. I asked him what he thought was fair, and he said, "Well, when you get a new car, could I have your used BMW Z3 sports car?" I asked if that would make things completely even, and he immediately said it would. So we made a deal. And again, for goodness' sake, everyone was happy.

Slipups in the quest for equal sibling treatment can be devastating. I know of a family where the well-to-do parents decided to give one sibling a greater inheritance, since the younger sibling had married someone wealthy. The younger sibling was crushed, sensing punishment without cause, and felt that true parental love should result in equal treatment. Those types of decisions can create lasting hard feelings and bitterness.

So parents and grandparents, be vigilant at striving for equal treatment. And when in doubt, or in time of crisis, sometimes it works to ask the child what they think would be fair. And the cold, hard truth is that even with precisely equal treatment, one child may achieve greater success or happiness by virtue of time, chance, or their own actions.

The challenge of equal treatment is not always about money, but also time, help, moral support, and the way in which our gracious love is given. Parents must never express the thought that they prefer a certain child, or think one child is better, or more attractive, or more anything. "I love you all the same" has to be the unyielding mantra. Good luck, you crazy parents!

May 2020

A Day in the Life of COVID Lockdown

The world as we know it has changed, and virtually everywhere, the COVID-19 pandemic has brought both personal and economic suffering. During this time we are all trying our best to remain safe and sane.

This is a report from the front in Santa Monica, California, where my wife and I have been in lockdown since March 17, 2020, pursuant to the orders of California Governor Gavin Newsom. We are privileged and are not suffering the pain many are, but this is difficult for all of us. Normally, my wife and I would be at our permanent residence at Lake Okoboji, Iowa, but we have decided this is not the time to do our usual four-day drive from California to Iowa with our two Labrador retrievers, Marge and Homer. Since I am seventy-one and my wife is seventy, we are in the danger zone with the virus, and we are being very careful. The only time we go out is to the pharmacy, the bank, or to do pickup at our local small grocery store. We are supposed to wear masks and we do. What follows is a typical day for me.

April 19, 2020

8:00 a.m.

Although my wife and I are mostly retired, I joke that we still get up at the crack of 9:00 a.m. But today Janet has an in-home workout class online that begins at 9:00, so I hear her alarm at 8:00. I roll over and sleep a bit more.

8:45 a.m.

I stumble out of bed, go to the bathroom, wash my hands for two singings of "Happy Birthday," brush my teeth, use the water pick, and don some cotton shorts and a T-shirt. I then grab my iPhone and put my medications in a Dixie cup. I decide I will shower later after my bike ride.

9:00 a.m.

I go downstairs and turn on the Keurig coffee maker, slice myself half a grapefruit, and then go out and get the three newspapers we have delivered to our door: the *Los Angeles Times*, *The Wall Street Journal*, and the *Financial Times* (an English newspaper).

9:15 a.m.

I toast an English muffin, butter it lightly, and sprinkle with some cinnamon sugar. My first cup of coffee is ready, and I have sectioned the grapefruit half, so I settle in to a very leisurely breakfast and check my emails as a first order of business. Today I find a couple of emails about our farm we operate in Missouri. The soybean and corn markets have collapsed, but fortunately we sold a good deal of our grain before the prices dropped. I also have an email from one of my law clients. When I was full-time in my law practice, I would look forward to calls or emails from clients, since it meant money. Now I am offended that they would disturb my morning by having the audacity to seek legal advice from me. I also have, as I do most days, about three or four emails from friends with jokes, videos, and god knows what.

9:45 a.m. to noon

I now continue breakfast and first grab the *L.A. Times*. I very briefly look at the front page to see the local news, check the new infections and the deaths, and see if any new lockdown rules are in the works. The current lockdown urges people to stay home and to venture out only for essential business. Next, I do the word jumble in the *L.A. Times*, then read the sports page, which has been relegated to a couple of pages in the "California" section. I check out the old sports replays that will be on TV to see if there is a good old World Series game, Super Bowl, or NBA championship game of interest.

Then I move to *The Wall Street Journal*. I read nearly every article in the first section, and then a few in the second section. I focus on the editorial page and other articles of opinion. I check out the ravages the virus is causing in our lives, read what is happening in other countries, and in business.

Next comes the *Financial Times*, which is an outstanding paper and provides a more European view of the news of the world. I am hesitant to ever discuss politics (or sex or religion) in A Distant Mirror, but I will say that I read a very liberal left-wing paper (the *L.A. Times*), a very conservative paper (*The Wall Street Journal*), and a cosmopolitan European paper that is somewhere in the political middle (the *Financial Times*).

Some people feel the day drags during a lockdown, but for me it does not. I feel like I have just been reading the papers for a bit, and damn if it is not noon already.

Noon

At noon, I will go into my home office and return emails—some personal, some farm related, and some seeking legal advice. I will have a client call maybe once or twice a week, but mostly I can answer the law questions by email. On Wednesdays, we have a farm conference call with our farm manager and our son, daughter, and son-in-law, all of whom help us with the farm business.

1:30 p.m.

At this time I make a cup of hot green tea, grab the book I am reading, and either sit at a table in our living room or at a table in our backyard and read for an hour, or two, or three. I may have a light lunch while reading, maybe an apple, maybe some soup, or if I ate a big breakfast, maybe nothing. The absence of sports has given me much more precious time to read.

Since March, I have read James Michener's *The Source*, Raymond Chandler's *The Big Sleep* and *Farewell, My Lovely* (Chandler is the dean of detective writers in my view), Shakespeare's *The Merchant of Venice*, and the first third of *The Pickwick Papers*, by Dickens. For the last week or so, I have been reading a particularly timely book, Stephen King's *The Stand*. I think it is by far King's best novel, one that I rank very high among my favorites. It tells a postapocalyptic tale of a deadly virus that escapes from a U.S. scientific lab and kills 99.4 percent of the people in the world. The few who are immune try to survive, living off all the clothes, food, and gasoline still sitting in stores now abandoned. I highly recommend the book.

3:30 p.m.

Time for my bike ride. Our neighborhood in Santa Monica is mainly a grid pattern, much like Grand Island, and very good for bike riding. With stores and businesses mostly closed, there is little traffic.

Today I first go east and circle the Brentwood Country Club, then head west down to Ocean Avenue, which is right on the coast and provides a beautiful view of the Pacific Ocean. Then back to 24th Street. My ride takes about forty-five minutes. I wear a mask. I see others out walking dogs or running or biking, but people are careful to keep their distance.

4:15 p.m.

I now grab another cup of hot green tea and read a bit more. At about this time, I also end up talking with friends and family on the phone. I have gotten a remarkable number of calls from friends with whom I do not regularly speak. Everyone is being kind and checking on each other. I think we are all desperate for a little social action and connection. We also FaceTime my daughter, son-in-law, and our two grandkids. This, of course, is a joy. My granddaughter will be ten years old on May 10, and she will likely have a virtual, or "Zoom," party, given that Minnesota is also on lockdown. I just sent her some Harry Potter books on CD. This will be the first birthday of hers at which I will not be physically present. Bummer.

5:00 p.m.

Now I make myself a bourbon, maybe get some almonds or fruit, and either do some more reading or watch the replay of some old sporting event or an old movie I have recorded.

6:30 p.m.

Janet is an excellent cook, and while I greatly miss my favorite Mexican restaurant, El Cholo, I am blessed with great meals at home. We will order food to be delivered maybe once or twice a week. We generally eat in our family room and first watch *Jeopardy!* then maybe a favorite old movie or something on Netflix, like *The Crown*, which we have been watching. One of my dirty little pleasures is to watch *Survivor*, so Wednesday is an exciting night.

9:30 p.m.

At 9:30 or 10:00 p.m. I will fall asleep in front of the TV downstairs, then go up to our bedroom and watch some more TV or read until I again fall asleep and get into bed.

While my schedule is not terribly demanding, from time to time I feel this mild sense of doom. When will this all end? When will I see my grandchildren? When will my beloved sports return to my life? When, as a seventy-one-year-old, can I feel safe to go out in the world? Time will tell, but until then, as the British say, "Keep calm and carry on!"

July 2020

Close Encounters With Celebrities

From 1976 to the present, my family has lived in the Brentwood and Santa Monica areas of Los Angeles, although since about 2012 we have split the time between our Santa Monica house and our house at Lake Okoboji, Iowa.

I am not a Hollywood guy, and I am not good friends with any Hollywood stars. Nor do I hang in such circles. But anyone living in the L.A. area for over forty-four years is bound to have crossed paths with celebrities just going about normal life. These "close encounters," if you will, are always sort of interesting, and sometimes quite fun.

Over the years I have been in restaurants and seen as fellow diners Bob Newhart, Mel Brooks and his wife, Anne Bancroft, Henry Winkler, Tom Petty, Ben Affleck, and Arnold Schwarzenegger. At

Peppone in Brentwood, my favorite Italian restaurant, I have seen Dustin Hoffman, Larry Flynt (in a wheelchair), and a very drunk Charlie Sheen, carrying on loudly outside the entrance to the restaurant.

The Arnold Schwarzenegger sighting was maybe sixteen years ago at a local breakfast place. With me were my daughter, my niece Erica, and four of Erica's college friends, who were staying at our house on spring break from Colorado College. There was Arnold, with his family, having eggs Benedict. All five of the college girls with me then had to go, one by one, to the bathroom so they could pass by his table and get a better look. They then got a double whammy later that day, when they again saw Arnold when they were Rollerblading along the bike path at the beach.

In classes at the spin studio near our house in Santa Monica, I have seen Helen Hunt, Will Ferrell, Calista Flockhart, Kevin Bacon, Kyra Sedgwick, Jennifer Grey ("Nobody puts Baby in the corner," from *Dirty Dancing*), and Brooke Shields.

The Brooke Shields encounter occurred when I was at a spin class taught by Tracy, my favorite teacher. I was spinning on the bike next to Tracy's husband, Mike, who is a TV anchorman for an Australian TV station. As the class ended, my friend Mike saw a woman walking out whom he knew and asked her why he had not seen her at his wife's class recently. The woman said her children were taking up much of her time. I then piped in and joked, "Well, what is more important, Tracy's class or your children?" She then laughed and proceeded out of the class. I turned to my buddy Mike and asked who that was. He looked at me strangely and said "Brooke Shields." I had not even recognized her.

In the late 1970s, one of my partners did law work for Jerry Mathers (the Beaver), and I met him briefly at a party. At a small grocery store near our Brentwood house, I saw Katharine Ross (*The Graduate*) checking out in front of me. She seemed more petite than I would have guessed, but beautiful, and was getting just a few items, including a pint of vanilla Häagen-Dazs ice cream. In that same small market, I once saw a huge man entering, who upon second look was Wilt Chamberlain.

We have close friends from Australia, including teenage twins, a boy and a girl. During a visit a couple of years ago, I took them to a Los Angeles Kings hockey game. The twins immediately recognized the actor Eric Stonestreet, from the TV show *Modern Family*, sitting near us. Once again, I would never have recognized him. They asked him if he would take a picture with them, and he graciously agreed. It made their day.

About twenty-five years ago, my wife, son, and daughter and I were leaving a Mother's Day brunch at the Café Four Oaks, a cute rustic place tucked into a leafy wooded area in L.A.'s Benedict Canyon. As we waited for our car from valet parking, a fancy new Range Rover pulled up. I then saw emerging from the car Warren Beatty and his wife, Annette Bening. They first had to extricate two young children from car seats. I am a huge fan of both Beatty and Bening, and, as I was later told, I apparently stood dumbfounded, staring with wide eyes and open mouth at their presence. Beatty saw me, smiled, and warmly asked me, "How are you?" I sprang to life, smiled, and said, "Fine, and you?" He smiled and said "Fine." Both of my kids later told me, "Dad, you were staring like an idiot." Apparently I was.

Roughly forty years ago, my wife, Janet, and daughter, Susannah, had an encounter in which I was not present. Janet was taking our four-year-old daughter to the doctor. They entered the elevator, in which there was another man. My daughter was loudly singing words from "My Life," the Billy Joel song she had just heard on the radio. She belted out, "I don't care what you say anymore this is my life!" At that point the man in the elevator then smiled and sang out, completing the next lyric, "Go ahead with your own life and leave me alone!" Janet looked up to see a very handsome man, with blazing blue eyes. It was Steve McQueen. McQueen then commented on what a cute little blond girl my daughter was. Janet was blown away.

But my favorite close encounter was with one of my favorite rockers, Rod Stewart. In 1990, I coached my ten-year-old son's Little League Baseball team at the Brentwood park where the park director was none other than my high school classmate, the late Mike Parmley, GIHS class of 1967. After our team's game, I stayed with another friend to watch the next game between two other teams in our league. One of the ten-year-olds playing in the second game was Rod Stewart's son Sean Stewart. I then saw Rod Stewart, with his first wife, Alana, sitting in the bleachers. In law school, eighteen years earlier, I probably listened to Stewart's *Never a Dull Moment* album about a hundred times. I particularly loved the song "You Wear It Well." So, while standing with my friend David Bordeaux behind the backstop, maybe twenty feet away from Stewart, I got frisky. I began to sing, fairly decently I might add, the first stanza of "You Wear It Well."

David began to cackle with laughter, and I looked over and saw Rod Stewart smiling broadly and also laughing. He gave me a quick little wink. I cannot help but chuckle every time I think of that one.

But I have to admit, the most amazing "close encounter" in my family did not involve me or my children, and it did not occur in California. Rather, it happened to my wife, Janet, in about 1956 in East Prairie, Missouri. Janet was about six years old when her parents took a trip to New York City to see some plays and enjoy the city. Janet stayed with their housekeeper, who lived across the street from the grandmother of Elvis Presley. The housekeeper's husband and son had recently died in a tragic trucking accident, and her grandson, about five years old, was living with her. While Janet and the lady's grandson were playing, they looked across the street and saw several large moving vans unloading a variety of appliances—TVs, a refrigerator, a stove, and much more. Elvis, who had just made it big, was treating his grandmother to some nice gifts.

When Janet and the young boy saw the empty boxes out front, they asked if they could play in the boxes, and they proceeded to do so. A bit later, when back at the housekeeper's house, they saw Elvis approaching. Elvis had heard of the tragic death of the husband and son, and he came over to pay his respects to the lady. He also brought over a toy fire truck as a present for the boy. But he did more than that, since he stayed for about an hour and played with Janet and the boy. Indeed, Janet remembers that Elvis actually put her on his shoulders and ran around the room, much to her delight. The King! Janet not only got to see him, in his prime, but also got a shoulder ride. Not surprisingly, Janet is still a major Elvis fan to this day.

November 2020

Wayne Monk, War Hero

On November 11, our nation celebrated Veterans Day. Today's Distant Mirror is a tribute to our veterans. In particular, I will today peer back into the 1940s and World War II. I know many GIHS alums have fathers, grandfathers, great-grandfathers, female ancestors, and many others who participated in the war effort in World War II. More than 400,000 Americans died in World War II. Countless other soldiers were heroes and served with valor.

    I cannot tell every story of the war experiences Americans had, but I can tell the story of my father, Wayne Virgil Monk. I do not suggest that he was anything but typical of our courageous soldiers, but his story is the one I know best. I am in part inspired to write about him since my brother Scott just located a copy of his honorable discharge papers.

I knew that my father had fought in Italy in World War II. But throughout his life he never once talked to me about his war experience until about a year or two before he died. Then, one day in 1989 or so, I asked him about it, and he talked for almost two hours.

He was inducted into the army at age eighteen from Elm Creek, Nebraska, on June 7, 1943, and entered active duty as an infantryman. He told me his squadron of two hundred men was first sent to Casablanca, Morocco, and then to Italy ("It-lee," as my father pronounced it). He fought in the Italian campaign, and specifically the Battle of Monte Cassino. Monte Cassino (between Naples and Rome), the site of a Benedictine monastery, was a high mountain position held by the Germans and was a key position in the Axis Gustav Line. This battle marked one of the longest and bloodiest engagements of the Italian campaign. The capture of Monte Cassino resulted in over 55,000 Allied casualties. The German losses were estimated at 20,000.

My father was in the historic Thirty-Fourth Division, which included Hawaiian and Japanese Americans who were not permitted to fight in the Pacific. He remained good friends with a Hawaiian fellow soldier throughout their lives after the war.

He said he lived and fought in a foxhole at the bottom of Monte Cassino for weeks after weeks. He said in this dirty, cold, smelly foxhole he ate, slept, defecated, was rained upon, and lived with dead soldiers near him for days. He said if you even once accidentally put your head up above the foxhole, you were likely to be killed. He said you didn't fear dying, you expected to die. What you feared was being horribly disfigured and then living.

My father then told me that of the 200 soldiers in his squadron, he was one of only 20 to survive the war; 180 men in his squadron died. He was eventually wounded on May 31, 1944, getting shrapnel in his back and earning a Purple Heart. He was then sent to Marseille, France, for a desk job for the remainder of the war.

He said when he got home to Elm Creek, for about a year or so he just drifted. He said no one could possibly understand what he had seen or been through, and he didn't want to talk about it. The amazing thing is that throughout his life, I never saw one ounce of bitterness or the mental scarring you might expect. My dad, nicknamed "Pickle," was the nicest guy in town, a total optimist, with a great dry sense of humor and was everyone's friend.

Near the end of the war, my grandfather, Perly Monk, received a letter from a war buddy my dad had fought with, which was published in the *Elm Creek Beacon*. The letter reads:

Somewhere in France,
December 10, 1944

Dear Mr. Monk:

I'm not good at this kind of writing but I'll try to explain. I am sending a $10.00 money order under your son's name and if you can't cash it please send it to him, and also send him my address. When he and I were in Italy he loaned me ten bucks, so I am paying him back.

Your son was in the same Bull-Head division I was in and I heard <u>lots</u> of good remarks about your son. He once saved his squad leader's life on a patrol. He was the last one to pull out and he helped the wounded all out of the tight spot. Wayne is a friendly type boy and everybody liked him well. When our boys went into combat with the 34th we never found a better division. After the war we're going to have a 34th day in Hawaii. He will be treated with the best of care. I'd like to thank Wayne, so will you please tell him thanks for me.

Alohe and best wishes,
David K. Gusnikon

My father's honorable discharge document has some other interesting details:

MILITARY OCCUPATIONAL SPECIALTY: Cable Clerk
MILITARY QUALIFICATION: MM rifle 26 Jul 43
BATTLES AND CAMPAIGNS: Rome-Arno, Rhineland, and Naples-Foggia
DECORATIONS AND CITATIONS: EAME service medal with 3 bronze service stars – Purple Heart Medal. GO 84 Hq 121st Gen Hosp 28 Jun 44 – Good Conduct Medal GO 47 Hq 135th Inf 5 Aug 44
WOUNDS RECEIVED IN ACTION: European Theater 31 May 44
DATE OF INDUCTION: 7 June 43
DATE OF SEPARATION: 4 Nov 45

What stunned me the most was that my father was one of only twenty of the two hundred in his infantry squadron who survived the war. If he had not, I would not be here. But the profound sadness is that 180 of the men in that squadron did not survive and did not live to return home to start, or return to, their families.

My California friend Bill Creim tells the story of his father in the Pacific theater in World War II. As an engineer, Bill's father had to be put ashore after a Japanese island was invaded to help build a quick, simple airfield to allow the Allies to land planes. One night Bill's father's Seabee unit was sleeping, dispersed in three large huts they had built as quarters for themselves. They were bombed, and two of the huts were destroyed, killing most of the men in those two huts. By sheer luck, Bill's father was in the hut that wasn't hit and awoke to find himself now in charge, as the higher-ranking officers were all killed. Once again, time, chance, and serendipitous events have such a significant impact on our lives.

When I hear these stories, I find myself wondering if I could ever have shown the courage that these soldiers displayed? Could I have endured and survived such horrific events? I am told that one's natural tendency toward self-preservation is overcome by the need to support your fellow soldiers and have their backs, and that sentiment generally carries the day.

Once again, I know there are thousands who have similar stories of their family members' heroism not only in World War II but in the Korean War, the Vietnam War, the Gulf War, and many other engagements on behalf of our country. Bless them all. May we never forget what they accomplished. May we forever be thankful.

January 2021

Fun and Games With Children and Grandchildren

From time immemorial, parents and grandparents have played games with their children and grandchildren. These games often evolve organically and are part of the joy and fabric of these relationships. Probably most readers have had such experiences either as a parent or child or both, and they are always interesting to me. So I share some of my experiences both as a parent and grandparent.

Bad Guys and Superheroes (1982-1984)

This was a game I played with my daughter, Susannah, and son, James, starting when they were about six and three years old, respectively. The basic premise was that Dad (that's me) was a Bad Guy, and they each were a Superhero. Many a night I would arrive home from work and hear them plead, "Dad, can we play Bad Guys and Superheroes?"

Susannah would usually choose to be either Wonder Woman or Supergirl. And she would try to wear her "Underoos," underwear that featured pictures of either Wonder Woman or Supergirl. There were some tense moments some mornings when Sue could not find some Underoos set to wear to school. It was a high-level crisis. But we would search the newly clean laundry, or sometimes even the dirty clothes, for one of the prized sets of underwear.

James would be a variety of heroes. Sometimes Ram Man, sometimes Superman, and sometimes others. I would be a generic "Bad Guy," but while playing, James would often call me "Zod, Bod, the Big Fat Hod" a phrase of mysterious origin.

The basic premise of the game was that I would chase them and attack them with pretend thrusts, parries, and other blows. They would fight back with their superpowers. They would blast with imaginary guns or weapons, or simply do a fake punch, which would cause me to fall back in agony. I would attempt to grab or punch or squeeze them, but they were quick at avoiding the Bad Guy. Also Ram Man would often literally "ram" me, and I would again fall back in agony. James also inserted the concept of a "force field," which he had seen in some movie. When I would be about to grab or get him, he would declare, "FORCE FIELD!" and if I got near him, I would scream in pain when my hand touched the invisible, but painful, force field.

Karate (1984-1987)

There was a period where James was interested in karate and was taking lessons. When he was about five or six years of age, every night I would come home from work and James would be there saying, "Dad? Can we?" And I knew he meant "can we fight and play karate." So usually we would. Basically, we would do hand whacks and kicks. The thrusts were mostly pretend, but some blows would land on the target, and we had some pretty rough-and-tumble battles. One day James was talking to a guest in the house, and he said, "I really like roughhousing." I don't know where he heard the phrase "roughhousing," but he knew it.

Olympic Diving (1984-1986)

In 1984, when the Summer Olympics were in Los Angeles, I took a two-week vacation and bought as many tickets as possible. My cousin Randy Garroutte (GIHS class of 1970), his wife and father-in-law, and my law school buddy John Fowler and his family all stayed at our house in Santa Monica and joined us at Olympic events. We saw tons of events, including the start of the first Olympic women's marathon ever, which at mile two went down San Vicente Boulevard, less than two blocks from our home in Santa Monica. During the Olympics, Bill, Randy's father-in-law, took our daughter, Susannah, to the female platform diving event, and that made a big impression.

Later that summer, when we were on the dock at Lake Okoboji, now our Iowa home, we developed the game of Olympic Diving. I would be the announcer, and I would say something like, "Next up from Sweden is Inga Gustafson!" Sue would then approach the end of the dock and do a crazy jump into the water, sometimes with twists and turns. Then I would solemnly and loudly announce, "The judges give it a 9, a 9, an 8, a 10, and the judge from the Soviet Union, a 3!"

I would next announce, "From Japan, the next diver is Yoshihiro Yamagi." James would then dramatically approach the end of the dock and do an equally crazy dive, can opener, or cannonball. I would then again announce, "And the judges give it a 9, a 10, an 8, a 9, and the judge from the Soviet Union, a 2."

Then I would approach the end of the dock and say, "Now up is Vassily Romanov, from the Soviet Union," then I would do a bad can opener or a "flying goose." While still in the lake I would shout, "The judges scores are a 3, a 4, a 4, a 2, and the judge from the Soviet Union, a 10!"

Bad Kitty! (2017-2020)

Fast-forward about thirty years, and I now play games with my grandchildren, Victoria, now ten, and Leonardo, now eight. Victoria has always loved cats and kitties. For something like five straight years on Halloween she was some kind of cat or kitty. Well, somehow that love morphed into the game of Bad Kitty.

I, Grandpa Mike, am the Bad Kitty. Victoria and Leo are little Good Kitties. Bad Kitty is required to remain in his chair, and Good Kitties try to come as close as possible and pester Bad Kitty, without Bad Kitty getting them. If Bad Kitty captures one of the Good Kitties, he either gives them a belly blow or, in a phrase my father used to love, he will "kiss them on the dirty neck." Bad Kitty starts the game by saying in a very scary voice, "I am a really Bad Kitty and I am going to get you!!" They then dodge around and try to poke me, but not get close enough to be caught. Sometimes Bad Kitty will pretend to be a Good Kitty and say, "Oh, I am just a very nice kitty and I would never hurt anyone. Come see." But they are too smart to come too close. On occasion, Bad Kitty is permitted to get out of the chair and chase them. But with these rules, there about a million "safe" places they can go, where Bad Kitty cannot get them.

A few years ago, we rented a suite at Target Field in Minneapolis for a Twins game. Victoria had invited three or four of her eight-year-old buddies, and she suggested we all play Bad Kitty. So I chased them around the suite in menacing fashion producing screams of joy and fear. Then, Mary Lazarus, our longtime friend from college days, joined the game as a female Bad Kitty. So two Bad Kitties were chasing the girls. Mary then developed the concept of "Sparkle." If a Bad Kitty is about to catch them, they get to yell "Sparkle," which freezes Bad Kitty. After playing for quite a while, we rested and I watched a little of the baseball game. Then Eva, one of Victoria's friends, came up to me and pleaded, "Can you chase us again?" Of course I did.

Sharkie and Fishies (2018-2020)

This is a game Victoria and Leo and I play in the pool at our Santa Monica house. I, of course, am the Sharkie, and they are the two Fishies. Sharkie swims around and tries to get them, and they swim away to avoid being caught. Once again, the Fishies are in a safe zone if they are touching the side of the pool, where Sharkie cannot get them. Since Victoria swims faster than I, she always gets away. And Leo carefully clings to a side of the pool if Sharkie is anywhere near. I don't know what Sharkie would do if he were to catch them, since he never has.

Crushing Machine and Other Machine Games (2016-2018)

From my buddy Jeff Greenberger (GIHS class of 1967) and his brother Dan (GIHS class of 1970), I have also learned a few new "Machine" games. One is the Crushing Machine, where one gets behind a grandchild and holds them very tight, a Crushing Machine. You have to be careful on this one not to crush too hard.

Another is the Upside-Down Machine, where I grab them by the feet and swing them around upside down. Yet another is the Washing Machine, where I hold them off the ground and shake them around like a washing machine. Each of these machines must be administered with care and caution. They generally produce laughter, but on rare occasions, a tear.

Some parents, I think, are hesitant to play such games, since they fear losing their dignity or are just not willing to be goofy and ridiculous. But for better or worse, I look forward to losing my dignity and being goofy and ridiculous. After all, you only live twice!

March 2021

Elmer Kral, English Teacher Extraordinaire

On January 21, 2021, former GIHS English teacher Elmer Kral passed away at age eighty-three. He taught at GIHS for twenty-six years, beginning in the mid-1960s. He was a true icon and legend in his own time. An extraordinary man and teacher, he left vivid memories with hundreds of GIHS students. I have heard amazing stories about him from numerous classmates and others whom he taught. Both George Ayoub and I have mentioned him in our writings for *Rise*, but I wanted to more thoroughly express my thoughts about Mr. Kral now. While I had many outstanding teachers at GIHS, Mr. Kral was unique.

Mr. Kral was my English teacher my senior year, from 1966 to 1967. A thin, bespectacled man whose shoulders slumped somewhat, he was physically distinct and very engaging. From the first day we walked into his classroom, we knew this would be a different experience. To start with, he referred to us by "Mr." and "Miss," with our last names. "Mr. Monk, Ms. Harrington, Mr. Hickstein, Ms. Dunham, Mr. Meedel." This new formality suggested we were adults. Further, discipline, effort, and organization were the orders of the day. He was demanding and fully prepared to call out a poor performer, either for lack of effort or poor attitude. He was not afraid to judge and rank students. This was not a class where every student got a trophy. Indeed, he seated his class by performance. The best performers were in the far right row, facing the front of the classroom, and the next best in the next row, and so on, until the far left row had the least successful performers. Even within those rows, he ranked each student's performance, with the best performer at the front of the row and so forth to the back of the row. And the seating could change with changes in performance.

He was probably best known for his focus and insistence on good grammar, good writing, and the correct use of commas, semicolons, and colons. My classmate Terry Virus recalled recently that Mr. Kral had thirty-three rules on commas and that these rules helped Terry get a top mark in English at the Naval Academy, even though he did not consider himself a great writer. We quickly learned that a sentence with two independent clauses needed a comma or semicolon to separate the clauses, while a sentence with two verbs connected by "and" did not. He attacked dangling participles, passive voice, and run-on sentences with vigor. Mr. Kral, in short, taught us to write well.

His focus on good writing extended even to spelling. While I had not had a spelling test since Howard grade school, we had spelling tests in Mr. Kral's senior English class. These tests expanded our vocabulary in addition to sharpening our spelling.

But Mr. Kral's most impressive achievement was that he not only taught the mechanics and rules of good writing, but he also conveyed and spurred a love of literature. We tackled some of the most challenging works in English literature, including Shakespeare's *Hamlet*, John Milton's *Paradise Lost*, and Jonathan Swift's *Gulliver's Travels*. We learned to appreciate and enjoy great literature.

Hamlet is considered by many to be the Bard's best and most complex play. We grew to appreciate some of the wonderful poetry:

The time is out of joint: O cursed spite,
That ever I was born to set it right!

and

To be, or not to be, that is the question:
Whether 'tis nobler in the mind to suffer
The slings and arrows of outrageous fortune,
Or to take arms against a sea of troubles,
And by opposing end them? . . .

Paradise Lost, published first in 1667 and revised in 1674, is also not an easy read. Milton's poem tells the story of Satan being ejected from Heaven and relegated to hell. Written in blank verse (iambic pentameter), it is erudite, complex, and long. One critic said while it is a fascinating and wonderful poem, no one ever wished it to be longer. Mr. Kral examined the religious, political, and poetic aspects of this great work. He also emphasized the true irony of *Paradise Lost*, which is that the most compelling, interesting character in the poem is Satan himself.

Mr. Kral was certainly demanding and, at times, quite stern. His stern behavior was never gratuitous, however, but always designed and meant to create better students and more successful human beings. I can still recall him saying to my classmate, the late and very bright Sue Ann Harrington, something to the effect of, "Miss Harrington, organization! How do you expect to be a success with such poor work habits?" To be late on an assignment or fail to study for a test would provoke a strong response.

But he also had a charming, playful side, and he would at times crack a painful joke. Even then, though, he consistently displayed a love of language and literature. One day Mr. Kral announced that Johnny Carson, who was then host of *The Tonight Show*, had declared that all limericks were dirty. Mr. Kral begged to differ, so he assigned us the task of writing clean limericks. He then sent the best ones on to the *Tonight Show*, but I don't recall that they were ever mentioned on the show. By the way, the most witty limerick, in my view, was written by none other than Sue Ann Harrington.

One day in class, my late classmate Mike George decided to try to stall the day's lesson. He asked Mr. Kral, in a very sincere voice, "Who do you think are the ten greatest writers in all literature?" Mr. Kral immediately took the bait. He started to review which writers should be on this list. "Well, let's see, I think Shakespeare would have to be number one. And *Paradise Lost* alone would put John Milton in the top ten." He went on to run through a dozen or so other likely top ten authors. Mike George just sat there, quietly grinning.

When I examined Mr. Kral's obituary, I was struck by how much he had accomplished apart from teaching. He wrote student term paper manuals and was a skeptical investigator of paranormal claims. He researched and wrote about distinguished Nebraskans, including the 2010 book *Profiles of Nationally Distinguished Nebraskans*, the 2012 work *Nationally Distinguished Nebraskans: A Bio-Bibliography of More Than 900 Individuals From 1854 to 2012*, and an internet document entitled "900 Famous Nebraskans." He also published five internet documents about Nebraskans of unusual longevity on the Nebraska Health Care Association website.

Mr. Kral was also very engaged with his hometown of Wilber, sponsoring a "Kral Room" at the Hotel Wilber, with historical photos. He also donated more than nine hundred photos of the history of Wilbur to the Nebraska State Historical Society. Beginning in

1995 he also established several scholarships and endowments, including the Robert Taylor Scholarship. Robert Taylor was a Nebraskan and famous Hollywood star about whom Mr. Kral did significant research.

I was greatly influenced and inspired by many GIHS teachers, including Judith Barth, Lillian Willman, John Heeckt, William Smith, Roger Harms, Gale Randle, and others. But Mr. Kral clearly had the most profound impact. I majored in English literature in college and became a lifelong fan of Dickens, Shakespeare, Jane Austen, George Eliot, the Romantic poets, and scores of other English writers. I eventually wrote a play in blank verse, in the style of Shakespeare, *The Tragedy of Orenthal, Prince of Brentwood*. The writing skills I learned from Mr. Kral have been invaluable in my forty-seven-year career as a lawyer.

About nine years ago, my class of 1967 was having its forty-fifth reunion. When we gathered the thoughts of classmates about teachers they had at GIHS, Mr. Kral was by far the most prominent recollection. My buddy and our class vice president, Jeff Greenberger, wrote Mr. Kral to invite him to our reunion. He wrote back a thankful letter but said his health would not permit him to attend. I think he signed this letter "E. A. Kral," noting that he had never liked the name Elmer but had continued to use it until his parents died. But now he was "E. A. Kral."

Also roughly eight or nine years ago, I realized I had never properly thanked Mr. Kral for all he did for me. I then wrote him a letter thanking him and emphasizing the profound impact he had on my education. I enclosed a copy of my play. He wrote me a touching letter in return, thanking me for my kind words and the recognition I gave him. He also praised my play and sent me in return a copy of his book on famous Nebraskans.

As I grow older, I attach great importance to recognizing and thanking those who did wonderful things for me. Mr. Kral is one of those people, and I treasure his work and memory.

May 2021

The Sport of Kings: Nebraska Horse Racing

Today we gaze into the Distant Mirror and look back to 1958, where we can examine the vibrant world of Thoroughbred horse racing in Nebraska, particularly at Fonner Park. In the late 1950s, there were three television channels to watch: KOLN Lincoln, KHAS Hastings, and a station from Kearney. There was one televised baseball game each week, one college football game each Saturday, and one pro football game per week. This was long before cable television, the internet, cell phones, and TikTok.

In this environment, when the horse races came to Fonner Park from late February to early April, the town was pumped with excitement. There was pageantry galore. There were beautiful horses, a well-manicured racetrack, colorful silks worn by the jockeys, the excitement of the paddock area, and the thrill of seeing your horse thundering down the stretch. Racing occurred every day but Sunday and Monday (I think), and it was a real social scene. At the track you would see friends, neighbors, teachers, bankers, laborers, doctors, farmers, business owners, and people from every realm of Grand Island society. For a $2 bet you could get a true adrenaline rush and maybe make some money. Once school let out in the afternoon, some high school students and even some teachers would rush to the track for the remaining races. In addition to Fonner Park, in the 1950s there were thriving racetracks in Columbus, Madison, South Sioux City, Lincoln, and Omaha.

My family was particularly intertwined with the racing scene. My late great-uncle Bud Bly owned horses for years. My uncle John Garroutte, who sadly passed away a few weeks ago, was involved with horse racing for over seventy years. As a young boy he rode horses in match races and at county fairs before his career as a professional jockey, riding in Nebraska, Oklahoma, Colorado, Louisiana, New Orleans, and New York. John then became an owner and trainer of horses. My late stepfather, Leon Hall, was also first a jockey, then a trainer and owner. Leon achieved some early fame as a leading jockey at a Chicago track at age fourteen, having lied about his age to be able to ride. Leon's father, Omar Hall, my brother Doug Hall's grandfather, was an owner and had a stable of very successful horses. Leon Hall and Omar Hall have both been inducted into the Nebraska Racing Hall of Fame. Many a Sunday dinner at our home would include horse-racing people as guests.

My uncle Bud would also take us to the barn areas where the horses were stabled, and we would chat with both the high and low of the business. When one of Bud's, or John's, or Leon's horses won a race, we kids would get to go onto the track and join them in the picture taken of the winning horse, jockey astride, surrounded by the owner, trainer, and family (see photo page 237).

Before he became an accountant for the state of Colorado, my cousin Randy served as a steward at Centennial Race Track in Denver. Stewards are the highest-ranking officials at a track and make the difficult decisions when fouls are claimed by jockeys and owners.

In addition to the joy of horse racing, I also saw some real tragedies. My uncle Bud had some very successful horses, including Bird Shooter and Heart Action. But his most prized and promising horse was Prince Dan. Just as Prince Dan was establishing himself as a true star horse, there was a horrific accident during a race in which Prince Dan ran into a fence and had to be euthanized. I know this brought tears to my uncle Bud's eyes. Also, my stepfather's dad, Omar Hall, had a number of outstanding horses that perished in a stable fire, and the loss was devastating to him.

My grandparents Doris and Raymond Dubbs were horse-racing fanatics. My grandfather worked long days as a section foreman repairing railroad tracks for the Union Pacific Railroad. But my grandmother, Bud Bly's sister, would usually go to Fonner each day of racing and bet my grandfather's standard daily double bet of five and seven. On most Saturdays during the racing season, my grandmother, grandfather, sister Pat, cousin Randy, aunt Cindy, and I would pile into one car and drive to Columbus or Madison or Lincoln to spend a day at the races.

As kids, we loved it. We would go to the paddock and watch the horses get saddled and watch the jockeys mount their horses. We would make bets and be thrilled when a bet made money. And a day at the track also meant popcorn, peanuts, hot dogs, candy, and cokes. My grandmother sharpened my math skills when she taught me to read a racing form at about age nine. We would always get a program, then examine the horses entered, the jockeys and trainers, and the "morning line" of betting odds. While I think the betting age was twenty-one, as kids we would always have Grandma make our bets for us. The excitement of getting back $3.80 on a $2 bet was enormous. Lots of kids would also pick up discarded tickets, since the occasional bettor would not realize that a show ticket had a payoff not only if the horse won, but also if the horse finished second or third. And some bettors mistakenly threw away good tickets. Every once in a while, one of us would find a good ticket, and that was manna from heaven.

Grandma told a story about one afternoon when she was driving to Fonner Park to make the first race and was stopped for speeding. The officer asked her why she was in such a hurry, and she replied, "I have to get to the track in time to bet the damn daily double." The officer laughed but wrote her a ticket, and she missed the daily double. Grandma always said the horse she wanted to bet in the first race that day was named "Stop Speeding."

As kids, we could sit with the grown-ups and enjoy the excitement and be part of the fun. The track we least liked to visit was Ak-Sar-Ben (Nebraska spelled backward), since at the Omaha track kids could not sit with those of betting age but were confined to the children's section, called the "Jr. Jockey Club," but somewhat like a jail. We called it the "pigpen."

When I got older, in high school, many of my friends would join me at the track, and the group generally centered around my wrinkled, but beaming, Grandma. She would hold court for a group that often included Mike Parmley, Bob Johnsen, George Ayoub, Mike Gearhart, Jeff Greenberger, my cousin Randy, and my sister Pat. Years later, my younger brother Doug Hall (GIHS class of 1978), Leon's son, and my younger cousin Jay Garroutte (GIHS class of 1978), John's son, would join the group. Since Grandma's brother Bud and her two sons-in-law were involved with racing, she gained a reputation as an "insider" who would have a good "tip." My friends would pump her for information, and she loved it. Grandma would opine, "Well, that Fred Ecoffey is a great jockey and you are taking a chance to bet against him. But I saw Bold Accent run in Lincoln last year, and that horse can run. And watch that horse owned by the Kemling brothers! Their horses always do well."

Grandma would often say something positive about nearly every horse in the race. And when the race was over, she would say, "Didn't I talk about that horse?" I would think, "Yes, Grandma, but you talked about all the horses." Grandma would occasionally bet on two, three, or even four horses in the same race. Then if one of her bets won, she would proudly pull the winning ticket out of her purse (not mentioning her losing tickets) and wave it high, with a big smile, saying, "I had that one!" Superstitions abounded. Some bettors favored a particular number, or a particular jockey or trainer, or a particular color of horse. My grandmother would often bet any "gray" horse in a race.

My cousin Randy Garroutte, even in junior high, was also deemed to be an insider who could provide a tip. One day when Randy was in class at Walnut, he was called down to the principal's office. Randy asked Agnes Ayoub, then working in the office, if he was in trouble. Aggie just said Johnny Hendricks, a counselor, wanted to see him. Randy walked into his office, and Mr. Hendricks immediately pulled out a racing form for that day at Fonner. He told Randy he needed help picking the second half of the daily double. He asked Randy, "Who do you like in the second race?"

In my high school and college years, a group of friends, plus my siblings Doug and Pat and my cousin Randy, and I would pool our money and do a "parlay," where any money we won would be placed back on a new bet. There were times where each of us might win ten dollars or so, a fortune to us. Then we would go together to Dreisbach's and eat like kings and queens with steak, chicken, fries, coleslaw, and other delights.

This early experience with horse racing and the jockeys, owners, and trainers taught me some important lessons. The first and foremost was that, in the long run, you cannot win with gambling. The obvious fiscal reality that more money is bet than is returned in winnings was part of it. But also, I saw the people who knew these horses well and who knew all the intricacies of the business and the local jockeys, trainers, and owners. But I saw vividly that while some of these "insiders" did well, most were generally not getting rich, and indeed, some lived very modest lives, even sleeping on cots in the stables near the horses. I thought if these people can't figure out who will win, then how can even the attentive and studious bettor make money.

The way I like to approach gambling at the racetrack is first to identify an amount I am prepared to lose, assume I will lose it, and view that as payment for the thrill I get from the action and the fun of rooting for a horse. If I make bets and actually break even, I have had all the fun of the action for free. Even better, if I win money, I enjoy that even more pleasing thrill of the chase and winning. With this mindset, betting can be a lot of fun.

The world of horse racing has encountered financial difficulties in recent decades, but it is still alive. The new Nebraska legislation allowing casino gambling at tracks will be a boon to Fonner Park. It should provide bigger purses and reinvigorate the industry. The joy of a day at the track with family, friends, the pageantry, the betting, and the beauty of the horses and surroundings is something to treasure. So embrace Fonner Park and enjoy the Sport of Kings!

July 2021

Victoria's Stuffed Animal Wedding

I first learned of "The Wedding" from my eleven-year-old granddaughter, Victoria, when on May 15 she proudly announced, with a big smile, "Grandpa, there is going to be a wedding tomorrow!" She explained that her favorite stuffed animal, Rose, the turtle, was going to marry Gerald, her little stuffed giraffe.

I asked if they were in love, and Victoria quickly responded, "Yes, very much."

"Have they been kissing?" I asked.

"A lot!" Victoria let me know. She asked if I could come to the wedding, which was the next day. I of course said I would be there.

At age eleven, Victoria, a fifth grader, is very mature and sophisticated in many ways. For example, she wanted to be present when the movers came to move the family belongings to the new house her parents have recently purchased, saying she would like to see the "buff dudes" who move furniture. When a close friend of mine was about to have prostate surgery, I explained to her what a prostate problem was. She then exclaimed, so it is not "constipation," but "consti-*pee*-tion."

But she still retains many of the joys of being a little girl. In particular, she loves make-believe and imaginary fun, a passion I hope and expect she will never lose. She has about twenty-five stuffed animals that she often brings with her when she visits our house. This past year, she assembled them at a separate little table for Thanksgiving, Christmas, and Easter dinners. The only real pets she has had in her life so far are two turtles, "Tiny" and "Leafy." So her favorite stuffed toy became Rose, her little stuffed turtle, who was to be married the next day.

When I arrived the next day, I saw Victoria had created a little chapel at the end of a long blue aisle for the wedding couple to walk down to take their vows. A leftover birthday balloon of a kitty flew proudly from the little chapel. Lined up along the aisle of matrimony, and sitting on the couch in back, were about twenty of the little stuffed animals ("animalitos" as her father calls them). There were doggies, kitties, Woodstock, birdies, a lion, a tiger, a stuffed avocado, and many more. Also present for the ceremony was her American Girl doll Julie, who dwarfed the animalitos. Just beyond the marriage site was a small table set up with plates and fake food, with an adjacent dance floor, for the reception.

Victoria had written out the full words of the wedding ceremony, and she handed them to me. She explained that I was to be the minister and read the couple their vows. Victoria would move the wedding participants around and be their voices. Her eight-year-old brother, Leo, would be the crowd noise and helper.

The ceremony began with Victoria singing a song while Woodstock went down the aisle as the flower person, spreading actual flower petals on the bridal path. Next, Gerald the giraffe, the groom, walked down the aisle, muttering, "I am so scared!" As he did so, Doggie shouted, "Here comes the groom, skinny as a broom!"

With the excitement palpable, Rose, the bride, then appeared. She was wearing an elaborate green cape and a beautiful purple ribbon. The stuffed avocado walked her down the aisle, as Victoria and I hummed the "Bridal Chorus" wedding march, by Wagner—"Here comes the bride," and so on.

Then began the ceremony, as written by Victoria:

"We are gathered here today for a romantic wedding to bring Rose and Gerald together in holy matrimony. Gerald, do you take this lovely girl, Rose, to be your wife?"

Gerald quickly responded, "I do."

"And, Rose, do you take Gerald to be your everlasting husband?"

Rose also quickly answered, "Yes, I do."

"Then let the ring bearer bring forth the rings."

Victoria had actual rings that were then brought out by Doggie. Doggie first put a ring on Gerald's stuffed body and then placed a ring on Rose's stuffed arm.

I then declared, "I now pronounce you turtle and giraffe."

Victoria quickly interrupted, "No, Grandpa, husband and wife!"

I then corrected myself, saying, "I now pronounce you husband and wife. You may now kiss the bride."

Then Rose and Gerald kissed for about a full minute, with Victoria circling them in the air and again humming the wedding march. Then they walked back down the wedding aisle.

Victoria then went around to each of the animalitos attending the wedding and had them do flips, shout out best wishes, and say things like, "You go get 'em!" and "Party on, dudes!" and "Yeah!"

There was, however, some small drama. One stuffed animal, a grouchy bird, declared, "This is utterly unacceptable." Also, when I suggested Tiger be the first to kiss the bride, Tiger flatly refused to kiss the bride, saying, "No, I broke up with her."

Then the newlyweds left the chapel. Victoria opted not to go with rice as they did so. They were then driven to the reception table in Leo's old toy dump truck, with Doggie driving and saying, "Yeah! Let's get this party started!"

Upon arriving at the reception table, before they could eat, Victoria had Rose and Gerald dance for quite a while, twirling around up in the air. Since Gerald is Leo's stuffed toy, at the end of the ceremony, Leo said, "Oh, I am so proud of my son!"

We of course recorded the wedding with a video. Victoria and Leo both thought the best part of the video was at the end, when one animal's shoe came flying in from off camera.

The reports after one week of marriage were very positive. Victoria said, "Yes, they are kissing a lot."

This wedding not only brought me joy, but it reminded me of Victoria's mother. In 1984 or so I came home from work and found my daughter, Susie, at age eight, with all of her stuffed animals seated together. She explained they were at school and she was teaching a class. But just when Susie would start to teach, Belle, stuffed Snoopy's stuffed sister, would disrupt class and require discipline. Is it genetic?

Further, Leo, my grandson, is not only a huge sports fan, but just this past year became very fond of Snoopy. Leo now has about three or four different stuffed Snoopys, plus a Snoopy calendar. Who knew?

September 2021

Middle School Socializing in 1964

As we gaze into today's Distant Mirror, we see a Friday night in January 1964. These were the days before cell phones, the internet, computers, cable TV, streaming, iPads, Facebook, Instagram, and all the cacophony of today's social media. People read newspapers as their major source of news. As a result, except for the occasional phone call or handwritten letter, socializing occurred in person.

On this Friday night, troves of junior high (there was no "middle school" then) students from Walnut and Barr are descending upon the GIHS gymnasium for the Friday Senior High basketball game between the Islanders and the Hastings Tigers. The gymnasium is packed, with parents, teachers, basketball fans of all ages, and many junior high and high school students. The pageantry is terrific.

There are perhaps one hundred girls in the GI Pep Club, resplendent in their purple uniforms, providing a visually strong and robust cheering section for the Islanders. The sounds, sights, and smells of popcorn and the gymnasium, with a band playing and spirited cheerleaders in prominent display, are mesmerizing.

For the students of Barr and Walnut, these were always special nights. The junior high students all sat together in the bleachers behind the basket nearest the entrance to the gymnasium. Groups of boys sat together, and groups of girls sat together. The groups provided protection, since for a girl to sit alone with one of the boys, or a boy to sit alone amongst the girls, would be a very bold step. It occasionally happened, but it took a very confident, or a very unwise, person to attempt it.

For these youngsters in that crucial developmental stage, this was high excitement. One might on occasion sit close enough to chat with a girl, and one had a chance to see all the pulchritude close up. Also, for the Barr and Walnut students in seventh through ninth grades, this was a rare chance to mingle with those from the other school. While you got to know the students from your own junior high quite well, you were usually less familiar with those from the other school. We all quietly assessed the attire, behavior, and personalities of individuals in the group, which boys and girls were the most cool, which the most humorous, which the most animated, and which the most unusual.

For me and many of the boys, this was not only a social opportunity, but a chance to watch your heroes on the hard court. This basketball was the big leagues for us. Very few college or pro games were televised then. As a result we all followed the Islanders closely. For the junior high students of 1964, when I was in ninth grade, our heroes were John Sanders, Lanny Martin, Art Glur, Dick Rezac, and others. We watched their every move and tried to pattern our play after these stars. Also, every GIHS basketball game was carried on radio, and you could follow the team on the road too.

For most of the junior high girls, the social aspects of the game were the most important. The chance to be around boys in a non-academic setting and to bond with your group of girlfriends was a big draw. I am sure that many of the glances thrown at the opposite sex in these games led to later romances in high school. This was, of course, before any junior high students had a driver's license, so dating had not yet started.

While the mixing of the boys and girls at an Islander basketball game was exciting, it was, of course, brief and merely the first step toward the more engaged social scene later in high school. Often, parents drove groups of junior high students to the game and drove them home afterward. Some of the older junior high students who lived nearby were permitted to walk to and from the game.

This was one of the limited occasions to mix with the opposite sex. There were of course others, including sock hops at the Walnut gym on Friday nights and dances at the YMCA, which were exciting. The first dance I remember in seventh grade was hilarious in retrospect. For at least a half hour, most of the boys stood along one side of the room and most of the girls along the other side of the room. Yes, wallflowers of both genders. Then a few girls might dance with each other. Finally, some girl might approach some boy and tell him that a particular girl would like to dance with him. With great trepidation, he might then approach the girl and ask her to dance. In the eighth and ninth grades, this shyness faded, and a more comfortable mixing occurred. And later there was the big Football Dance, at which a king and queen were crowned.

In my first days as a seventh grader at Walnut, in 1961, I had Mr. Epp for my block class, then walked up a flight of stairs to my next class. In my block class was a sweet girl named Dixie Davis, who was the only other student who had the same next class as I did. We on occasion began to walk to the next class together. Wow! Quite a thrill.

The first boy-girl party I ever experienced was actually in sixth grade with eight of my Howard School classmates. My buddy Jim Schroeder held a party at his house, with four boys and their "dates." My mother drove me to pick up my sixth-grade heartthrob, Kathy Gregory, and that was a new and wonderful experience. The eight of us nervously danced, chatted, and had sloppy joes for dinner before our parents came to drive us home.

There was also the roller-skating rink, where to skate around with a nice girl or boy was a real thrill. And of course the movies became a place for junior high boys and girls to gather. At the movies one might sit next to a girl, and the sexual tension might be high. But very little, if any, exciting activity occurred. The older junior high students eventually started having parties in private homes, and this was a major breakthrough. The parties were mostly giggling, munching some food, and listening to records, with a little dancing.

The days of real dates in cars were far way, just a faint vision of what might later come. But the thrill of these brief encounters as a young teen was immense.

As to high school dating, I have virtually no sense of what happens today. My children are in their forties and far from high school. My grandchildren are far from the dating scene at eight and eleven years old, so I have no source of information. I do sense that dating in high school in the 1960s was very different from today, however. At that time there was a dance at the YMCA after the Friday night football games, and these were terrific times. Also, many people dated, often just a couple, to go to the movies or get a snack at Nifty's or King's Drive-In. Things were casual, and we didn't view a date as a prelude to marriage or any serious involvement, but simply a chance to go out and have some fun. People dated not just one person, but many, although of course some couples decided to go "steady" with a single boyfriend or girlfriend. When my children were in high school in the 1990s, boys and girls tended to go out in groups rather than single "dates."

I know the charm and magic of those first social encounters will always survive. And they will, as you can tell from this writing, leave memories that will last a lifetime. I hope and expect that Islander basketball and football games continue to be a special time and a great chance to mix. That part of growing up in a small city in Nebraska will continue to bless and enchant us all.

November 2021

The Cake in the Face Case

Friends often ask me about the more interesting or amusing cases I have handled in my forty-seven years of law practice. My practice involves representing employers: I guide them on how to comply with the law, I provide counsel on whether certain conduct merits discipline or discharge, and I also defend lawsuits brought against employers by discharged employees. Of course, many lawsuits brought by employees have merit and seek to address unlawful actions. But I have seen a surprising number of cases where the employee seeks desperately to defend misconduct by raising false issues. The "Cake in the Face Case" is one such case.

This case involved actions by an employee of a nonprofit employer that employed social workers. The social workers did case management and helped provide resources to developmentally disabled persons. Social worker "Mr. Attacker" (the names have been changed to protect the innocent and the guilty) wanted to take a Friday off, even though he had a major matter occurring that day. One of the developmentally disabled persons in his caseload was being transferred to a new residence. Such a transfer is always a delicate and emotional matter for a vulnerable, developmentally disabled person. Mr. Attacker was supposed to be there to guide the process and smooth any bumps along the way.

But Mr. Attacker asked his work colleague "Mr. Victim" to cover for him on that Friday, since Attacker wanted a three-day weekend. Victim agreed to cover. While Victim did everything he could to assist in the transfer on that Friday, things did not go well. On Monday morning, Mr. Attacker's supervisor confronted him and reprimanded him severely for not handling the matter himself.

Attacker then became furious at Victim, since Victim had handled the matter, and the transfer to the new residence did not go well. That same Monday, there was a birthday celebration at the office. A cardboard platter with some cake remnants was left in the lunchroom. Attacker picked up the cardboard platter, approached Victim in the hallway, yelled at him, and called him a profane name. Victim ignored Attacker. Attacker, however, then approached Victim, shouted more profanity, and abruptly shoved the cardboard platter into Victim's face, smearing cake all over Victim and breaking the eyeglasses he was wearing. It was a violent act observed by several other employees.

Victim did not report this to management, but several other employees who had observed and were offended by the violence did report it. The human resources director then interviewed Victim, who confirmed the reports of what happened. The HR director then also interviewed Attacker and informed him that the employer had received reports that Attacker had (1) called Victim a profane name, (2) yelled other profanity at Victim, and (3) smashed the cardboard platter into his face, smearing cake all over Victim's face and breaking the eyeglasses Victim was wearing.

Attacker denied that these things had happened, telling a different story. Attacker said that after Victim saw the cake in the hallway, Victim called Attacker a "cheap Jew" for not offering him some cake. Attacker went on to claim that he then facetiously offered Victim some cake but that the platter of cake slipped and went into Victim's face by accident.

Several other employees and Victim all confirmed that Attacker's story was false and reiterated that Attacker had called Victim a profane name and violently shoved the platter in his face. No one heard any reference to a "cheap Jew." The company concluded that the weight of the evidence confirmed the observations of several employees and Victim. Accordingly, based on the violent physical attack and the misconduct associated with the encounter, the company discharged Attacker.

After being discharged, Attacker sued the employer, claiming religious discrimination, since he was fired after Victim called him a "cheap Jew." After the lawsuit was filed, I held a formal deposition and questioned Attacker about the facts of the case and his contentions.

> MONK: Do you believe you were fired for religious reasons?
> ATTACKER: Yes.
> MONK: So, Mr. Attacker, why do you believe you were fired because of your religion?
> ATTACKER: Because Mr. Victim called me a "cheap Jew," and I was thereafter fired because of my religion, despite this attack on my religion.
> MONK: Were you raised in a Jewish family?
> ATTACKER: No, a Catholic family.
> MONK: Did you ever convert to Judaism?
> ATTACKER: No.
> MONK: Do you regularly worship at a synagogue?
> ATTACKER: No.
> MONK: Have you ever been in a synagogue to worship?

ATTACKER: No.

MONK: Well then, why do you contend that you were discriminated against based on your Jewish faith?

ATTACKER: Well . . . I respect their traditions, and I like kosher meat.

MONK: So I suppose you love Mel Brooks movies too?

ATTACKER: No, as a matter of fact I don't.

Thereafter I brought a motion for summary judgment to dismiss the lawsuit. This motion argued that there was no credible evidence of religious discrimination. When I appeared in court that morning, the judge began by telling both lawyers that he was Jewish. He asked if either party had a problem with that or wished to remove him from the case. I immediately proclaimed, "No, Your Honor!" The lawyer for Attacker also grudgingly said he did not have a problem with the judge being of the Jewish faith.

Upon learning the judge was Jewish, I was delighted, since I did not think the judge would be amused by the manner in which Attacker had misrepresented his claim to be Jewish. After both counsel had made their arguments, the judge granted our motion for summary judgment, dismissing the lawsuit.

Cases such as this not only misuse the laws protecting against religious discrimination and other unlawful discrimination, but also taint those other cases in which employees are the true victims of religious or other discrimination. These cases no longer surprise me, since in the eyes of the employee who has lost his job, "desperate times call for desperate measures." But such cases not only demean those who bring such false claims, they also offend the important protections discrimination laws provide our society. But in this case, thank goodness, the Attacker was not able to commit the violent and aggressive actions he did and still remain employed. I think justice prevailed. Pretty much every employee wishes to work in an office where there will be no "Cake in the Face."

January 2022

The Golden Era of Pinball

Today, we gaze into the Distant Mirror and see Grand Island in the 1950s and 1960s, during the golden era of pinball machines.

At that time there was no PlayStation 5 (one of which my grandson, Leonardo, received for Christmas this year, to his open-mouthed delight). Neither was there Madden NFL Football, nor the vast number of games in the Apple App Store. There was not even Nintendo's Luigi or Mario, or even Pong.

But there was the lure of the pinball machine. A real game where you saw a real silver ball bouncing merrily between barriers, bumpers, and holes, whose collision with those barriers, bumpers, and holes was punctuated by lights, buzzers, and bells. The original machines had two flippers at the bottom to send the ball back upward for more points. You were given five balls with which to play. While getting a high score was one goal, the real treat was to win a free game, or replay, which the machine would confirm with a distinct knocking sound. In a very good game, you might hear successive knocks indicating multiple replays and producing great joy and excitement. You could push the machine just a bit to aid the progress of the silver ball toward scores or away from danger. But if you jiggled the machine too much, it would "tilt" and your game was over.

When playing pinball, the flashing lights, buzzers, and bells create a cavalcade of sound and visual excitement, adding to the tactile pleasure of the vibrations and the progress of the silver ball. First, you hear a soft plunk, and the first ball falls into place in the shoot on the right of the machine. Then you pull the plunger, and the ball rockets up the right side of the machine into play. The ball hits some bumpers and goes back and forth between them: *bampity bam, bam, bam!* Points are racking up and lights are flashing! Then the ball rolls down and you send it upward with a flipper. It enters a shoot and lands in a hole that adds more points: *ping, ping, ping . . . ding, ding, ding!* Then the machine shoots the ball down rapidly, which requires a quick flip upward. The ball bangs back and forth between the bottom barriers, almost going down the center, but you flip it back up, first with one flipper and then with the other. The silver ball then flies back up to the bumpers and more *bampity bam, bam, bam!* Finally, the ball falls between the two flippers and descends down the shoot. It is now time for the next ball. Engrossing, indeed!

Pinball machines were ubiquitous throughout Grand Island—at bowling alleys, grocery stores, the bus station, restaurants, and other locations. For a quarter, I think, you could get three games. Each machine had a theme, whether it was pirates, the circus, poker, car racing, or sports. There were color pictures on the board and on the upright display at the back of the machine. The artwork on the machines was fantastic, colorful, exotic, and, only rarely and to some small extent, prurient. Machines were made by Gottlieb, Bally, Williams, and other companies.

Online today, in fact, you can find vintage machines for sale. Not always cheap, but always intriguing, they include:

- a 1948 machine called "Yanks Baseball"
- a Gottlieb machine called "Ship Ahoy" with a nautical theme
- a Gottlieb machine called "Rack-a-Ball" with a pool table theme
- a 1953 Gottlieb machine called "Flying High" with an airplane theme and a scantily clad woman front and center
- a Gottlieb machine called "Royal Flush" with a poker theme
- a 1963 machine named "Slick Chick" with a group of people at a bar, including some slick chicks
- a Gottlieb machine called "Sinbad" with the Sinbad legend as the theme

Four locations at which I recall playing pinball were the Rockwell Bowling Alley on Second Street, the Greyhound bus station, the small local grocery store, Crick's, on North Wheeler Street, and the burger joint Ott's, a half block from the old Walnut Junior High campus, on Eddy Street near the underpass.

At Crick's, groups of youths would hang out, playing pinball, trying for free games, exchanging banter, eating candy, and drinking pop. Some small amount of decorum was required or you would be asked to leave the store.

I would often go with my mother, Ramona, to the Rockwell Bowling Alley to watch her bowl in the league in which she competed. While I would mostly watch her bowl, I would at times beg for a quarter and then drift over to the pinball machine near the entrance. This machine, called Tropic Isle, had a tropical paradise theme with luscious pictures of a beach and palm trees. Among other ways to score points, this machine had three monkeys that would successively climb a long, curved palm tree when points were scored. It took a bit of time for each monkey to get to the top, but when all three monkeys got there, you were rewarded with a bonanza of points and multiple replays. The intriguing aspect of this game was that the progress of each monkey up the tree was retained for the next game. So if you came upon a chance to play the machine when two of the monkeys were at the top and the third one nearly there, you had a great chance at the bonanza of points and replays.

Stunningly, I found a vintage version of this very Tropic Isle machine on sale online for only $3,095. If anyone is desperate to get me a late Christmas present, this would do nicely.

The little diner called Ott's was the scene of a bustling lunchtime crowd when Walnut was in session in the 1960s. Just a half a block down the street, past the Woitaszewski house, the place had outstanding burgers and the best french fries in town. The three or four booths were always packed, and the pinball machine at the back of the little shop was always busy. The big treat at Ott's was that if you won a replay, you not only got the replay, but also a free malt from the store. Wow!

One day I was in Ott's, and I noticed an older boy (maybe fifteen or sixteen), win a replay and a malt. As I watched closer, I saw he had ever so carefully lifted up the machine so the two front legs were resting on his shoes. This had to be done with great dexterity, or you would tilt the game. But if successful, this reduced the slant of the machine, so the ball was far easier to keep in play. I was astounded at the boy's audacity and the success with which he carried out his crime. I was also a nervous wreck that he would get caught in the act.

Today, the occasional original-type pinball machine is still out there, in arcades and bowling alleys. I found one at a bowling alley in Minneapolis and introduced my two grandchildren to the game. They would play at the same time with one handling the right flipper and one the left. After their move back to California, we recently found a machine in Camarillo, California, again at a bowling alley.

The glory and attraction of pinball was captured in the 1969 song "Pinball Wizard," part of the iconic *Tommy* album by The Who. While this terrific song is a fantasy, it still conveys the joy and fun of pinball. May the days of pinball live on forever!

March 2022

"Won't You Let Me Take You on a Sea Cruise?"

Despite this 1959 Frankie Ford song, for the first fifty-five years of my life, I never took a cruise. I viewed cruise ships and cruises as experiences for the geriatric, the fearful, and those unable to properly schedule their own vacations. My family and I were fortunate enough to take several European vacations in France, England, Italy, and Greece, where we would rent a car and drive to our desired locations. But we had never been on a cruise ship.

After our friends Mary and Barry Lazarus began to take cruises on the Crystal Cruises line, my wife, Janet, and I started to consider the possibility. So in 2004, for our thirtieth wedding anniversary, we decided to take a Princess cruise of the Baltic. We would have ports of call in Copenhagen, Denmark; Stockholm, Sweden; Helsinki,

Finland; Saint Petersburg, Russia; Tallinn, Estonia; Gdańsk, Poland; and Oslo, Norway. These were all places we had not visited. To be able to see them all on a two-week cruise seemed remarkable. To tour all these cities in a driving vacation would take far longer.

We really enjoyed the Baltic cruise. We were seated for dinners at a table of eight, with a couple from San Francisco about our age, a couple from Connecticut celebrating their fiftieth anniversary, and two lovely widows from England, in their sixties. All were engaging and charming.

Thereafter, having gotten the cruising bug, Janet and I have taken six additional cruises with our friends Mary and Barry and one cruise with our friends Steve and Nancy Sicher. These were all cruises with Crystal Cruises, on either the *Crystal Serenity* or the *Crystal Symphony*. These were midsize cruise ships carrying about nine hundred guests.

We discovered that cruises are quite pleasant. There is the great advantage of having to pack and unpack only once. The rooms are cozy but nice, with a private balcony overlooking the sea. While the stops and excursions are wonderful, even the days at sea, without a port of call, are delightful. If you wanted room service for breakfast you simply called for it. For a late afternoon drink and snack, you simply called for it. The ship had a well-equipped gym, a library, a computer room, a swimming pool, a movie theater, lecture halls, and a gambling casino. The evening included a lovely dinner, and afterward, there were live Broadway-type shows, a movie, or a visit to the casino.

During the day, in advance of a stop at a particular city, there would be lectures by experts touching on the highlights and history of the city we were to visit and describing the various excursions available from the ship. In addition, there were trivia contests, bingo, a golf simulator, and a shuffleboard area.

On our Crystal ships, the food was outstanding, with sit-down service, buffets, and specialty Asian and Italian restaurants. All food and alcohol were included in the cost of the cruise, and there was no tipping. Also, when cruising with friends, you always had dinner companions whom you enjoy. There was ample time to simply relax and read, either in your room, around the swimming pool, on deck of the ship, in one of the lounges, or in the library. On one cruise I read pretty much all of *Middlemarch*, by George Eliot.

Over the years, we took cruises of the Mediterranean, through the Panama Canal, to Alaska, to Hawaii, from Montreal to New York, and a cruise of the Danube River in Europe. Our most recent one was a cruise of the Greek islands in 2019.

During our 2004 Baltic cruise, at the Saint Petersburg stop, we toured Peter the Great's Winter Palace. Our young female tour guide emphasized on more than one occasion "that Putin is great and the country loves him very much." Both then and now, my thought was, "The lady doth protest too much, methinks."

One of the lectures we attended had a speaker who analyzed serial killers. He talked about their backgrounds, their commonalities, and other specifics. This presentation was fascinating, but not so fascinating that I didn't fall asleep sitting between Janet and our friend Mary. My sleep, however, was abruptly interrupted when I awoke to hear the entire lecture room, with maybe a hundred people, in uproarious laughter. It turns out they were laughing at me, at whom both Janet and Mary were pointing. The lecturer had pointed out that the most common trait among serial killers is having the middle name "Wayne" (John Wayne Gacy, for example). Well, of course, my middle name is "Wayne." So when the speaker asked if anybody in the audience had that middle name, Janet and Mary pointed to me, sound asleep, and the rest is history.

On our cruise through the Panama Canal, the highlight was seeing our large cruise ship go through the locks that raise and lower the ships as they progress through the canal. We also had a port of call on Saint John's in the Virgin Islands. There, we had an outing where we got to be a crew on a former America's Cup ship. Janet,

Mary, and I were on *True North*, a former Canadian entry in the America's Cup. We had a fun practice sail against a second yacht, the *Stars & Stripes*, a former USA entrant.

Our cruise of the Mediterranean included a stop on Sicily. We chose an excursion that took us to the very villa where a scene from the classic movie *The Godfather* was filmed. It was the villa where Michael Corleone was in hiding, with the courtyard in which his new wife is killed when the car explodes. It was extraordinary to see that location in person.

Another great day was when we got a private car to drive us around the Amalfi Coast in Italy. While the views were spectacular, our driver, like all Italian drivers, drove ridiculously fast. The narrow roads on the precipitous slopes of Positano were dangerous enough. But our driver was weaving in and out of heavy traffic, and for the first half hour, I thought we would die for sure. But after a while, I just went with it, and we did not die. At one point along the drive, he slowed down and waved to an oncoming bus driver. It was his brother.

On the same Mediterranean cruise, we had a port of call at Florence and took a particular excursion touring places in Florence mentioned in *The Da Vinci Code*.

On our Alaska cruise, we got to come surprisingly close to glaciers that were calving. Not only was it an extraordinary visual, but the sound of the calving was like a firecracker going off. Fascinating.

Suffice it to say, taking a cruise can be one heck of a lot of fun. It's like being in an all-purpose resort, with every pleasure you could desire, while simultaneously traveling from wonderful city to wonderful city. Unfortunately, Crystal Cruises did not survive the COVID pandemic. With most cruises canceled for a year and a half or so, they went out of business. But other cruise lines exist and are now ramping up. So, I ask,

"Won't you let me take you on a sea cruise?"

May 2022

Wonder Woman's Boots

In December 1980, I flew from Los Angeles to Omaha to return to Nebraska for Christmas. Since my wife, Janet, had teaching obligations that continued until just shortly before Christmas, I embarked to Nebraska with our two children several days early. My daughter, Susie, was four and a half years old and my son, James, just eighteen months old. Janet would join us later in the week.

I knew that this would be a serious parental sports challenge to fly with two young children by myself. But I thought I would be fine. I knew sometimes flight attendants were very solicitous of young children and would offer to help. But on this particular flight, every seat was taken. It was crowded. We had the window seat and the middle seat for the three of us, with James sitting on my lap. I soon discovered that I could not even get eye contact with any flight attendant. They were extremely busy, with no time to help a dad struggling with two youngsters.

Shortly after we were in the air, Susie declared that she had to go to the bathroom. So I proceeded to take her and James to the bathroom. I crawled around the man in the aisle seat, carrying James in my arms and taking Susie by the hand, and headed down the middle aisle to the bathroom. At that very time the flight attendants were starting to deliver drinks to passengers, so we had to dodge the drink cart. We finally got back to the bathroom. While holding James, in very tight quarters, I assisted Susie in going to the bathroom.

We returned to our seats, again having to navigate by the cart of drinks. We sat down and James began to cry. I comforted him, and after a while he was better, but still squirmy. Then they brought our food. I placed Susie's food on her tray table, and the food for James and myself on my tray table. I was trying to feed James when Susie declared, "Daddy, you need to cut my meat. Please cut my meat!" So between giving James some bites, I squirmed over and cut her meat. I spilled only a minor amount of food, and we eventually had a little something to eat. I began to relax.

But just as the flight attendants came around to pick up the trays, Susie again declared, "Dad, I have to go to the bathroom badly." So once again the three of us crawled over the man in the aisle seat and maneuvered back through the middle aisle of the plane to the bathroom, dodging the flight attendant picking up trays.

After Susie finished, we then trudged back to our seats, again getting by the man in the aisle seat. Susie then wanted to play with her new Wonder Woman doll. The doll, about the size of a Barbie doll, had superheroine clothing, a crown, and some shiny black plastic boots. Susie was enjoying playing with Wonder Woman, undressing her and then dressing her. Then she decided it was essential to remove Wonder Woman's boots. This was not easy, since they were a snug fit. Susie pulled and tugged. Then I pulled and tugged. Finally, Susie was able to rip one of Wonder Woman's boots off, which flew up over the passengers in front of us and landed somewhere about three rows up.

Susie began to panic. "Dad, Dad, I need Wonder Woman's boot! Where is Wonder Woman's boot? Get me Wonder Woman's boot!" I was penned in and holding James. I was not in a position to go searching for Wonder Woman's boot two or three rows ahead of us. But the need to find Wonder Woman's boot was great. Soon other passengers heard Susie, and the need to find the boot soon spread throughout our section of the plane. Thank goodness, a man three rows up found the boot and passed it back to us. The crisis was over. The other passengers were remarkably understanding. I do not even recall any dirty looks. Now Susie needed help to get Wonder Woman's boot back on, which was not easy while holding James.

James had been startled by the loss of Wonder Woman's boot, and he began to fuss and squirm. While he was fussing and crying, Susie announced, for the third time in the three-and-a-half-hour flight, that she had to go to the bathroom. So we repeated the bathroom ritual, with the usual difficulty. The flight attendants continued to avoid making eye contact with me so that I couldn't seek their help. But we did the job and got back to our seats. I had been hoping for the entire flight that James might fall asleep. . . . Finally, with about ten minutes left in the flight, he peacefully fell into slumber.

We soon landed, having finally arrived in Omaha. As I am sure many of you are thinking, the only one to blame for this difficult trip was yours truly. But, frankly, it was more than worth it, simply to have the story to tell. I have told the story to my grandchildren, Victoria and Leo, several times. It is one of their favorites. They love hearing about their mom's passion for Wonder Woman's boots. Sometimes out of nowhere they will demand that I tell the story again. I always enjoy doing so.

Five generations together, *clockwise, left to right*: Ramona Monk (Mom), Raymond Dubbs (my grandfather) holding me, Mrs. Donnie Dubbs (my great-grandmother), and seated, A. L. Watson (my great-great-grandmother).

My parents, Wayne and Ramona Monk, 1948.

My father holding me, with my grandparents Perley and Louise Monk.

My father in his army uniform, 1944.

My father, Wayne, 1942.

My mother, Ramona, c. 1949.

My mother, Uncle Max, and Aunt Jerenne, c. 1939.

My sister Patricia Wagoner and me, c. 1956.

The Winner's Circle picture after my uncle Bud's horse Bird Shooter won a race in 1958. *From far left*: my cousin Randy Garroutte, my sister Patricia Wagoner, and me, with my grandmother Doris Dubbs behind us. Uncle Bud is holding the horse.

Our Little League "Yanks" team in 1959. I'm in the front row, third from right. My cousin Randy is in the front, fourth from left.

A picture of the swimming school in Okoboji, circa 1954. Janet is in the middle of the bottom row, in the checkered shirt.

A 1960 picture of the Howard School Band, after appearing in the Harvest of Harmony parade. I'm in the back row, third from left. Peggy Burger is on my right. Kathy Gregory is in the white sweater on the left in the front row.

My sixth-grade class at the roller-skating rink in Grand Island, Nebraska, 1960. I'm the second from the right in the bottom row.

My ninth-grade basketball team at Walnut Junior High. I'm in the bottom row, second from right. Next to me, on the far right, is my buddy George Ayoub.

Dave Townsend and me after I was elected president of the Student Council in 1966.

Here I am in 1966 presiding as president of the YMCA and YWCA Inter Club Council.

At my induction into the Grand Island High School Hall of Honor with my high school classmates in 1992.

My daughter, Susie, with her one-year-old daughter, Victoria, on the day she learned to walk, in 2011.

Going through the Panama Canal on the 2012 cruise.

The view from True North while sailing in an America's Cup yacht, 2012.

The gang in Okoboji, 2012. *Standing, from left,* my cousin Randy; son-in-law, Caesar; daughter, Susie; friend Mary; brother Doug; sister Pat; sister-in-law, Patricia; Janet; and me. Victoria and our Labs, Marge and Homer, are in front.

My wife, Janet, with Bob and Donna Johnsen at a Padres game in 2013.

With Janet at the *Godfather* villa in Sicily, 2013.

With my buddy John Fowler at the 2013 World Series.

Leo and Victoria at a Minneapolis pool in 2014.

At the Formula One race with my son, James, in Austin, 2014.

James at the Formula One race in Austin, 2014.

After getting ice cream with Victoria and Leo in Minneapolis in 2015.

Leo kicking the soccer ball in Okoboji, 2016.

With Caesar and his brother Ricardo at Anfield stadium in Liverpool to see the match between Liverpool and Everton in January 2014.

Janet and I in Venice at the start of our Mediterranean cruise in 2013 with Mary and Barry Lazarus and Gail and Lou Bernucca.

Mary, me, and Janet posing with the character at the house of Anne of Green Gables in Prince Edward Island, Canada, 2015.

Dinner on the cruise ship with Janet and Mary and Barry Lazarus in 2015.

Budapest during our 2017 Danube cruise.

Hawaii, 2018.

Dying Easter eggs with Susie, Janet, and Victoria in Santa Monica in 2013.

Caesar, Janet, Susie, Leo, and Victoria in Minneapolis, 2014.

First day of kindergarten for Victoria in Minneapolis, 2015.

Victoria the ballerina in 2015.

Sledding in Minneapolis with Susie, Victoria, and Caesar, c. 2016.

Three generations of girls cooking: Janet, Susie, and Victoria in 2015.

With my brother Doug and sister Pat at my niece Erica's 2016 wedding.

Doug, Patricia, Pat, and me before a 2015 Nebraska football game.

Patricia, Janet, and Doug in Okoboji.

Susannah, Janet, me, and Victoria at the Guthrie Theater in Minneapolis after seeing *West Side Story* in 2018.

Clockwise: Me, James, Caesar, Leo, Janet, Victoria, and Susie at a pumpkin patch in Minnesota, c. 2018.

Leo after a soccer game in 2018.

With Leo at a Twins game in 2017.

Minnesota Loons soccer match in 2018 with Leo.

Vikings game in Minneapolis with Leo, 2019.

Leo and me at the 2020 Rose Bowl to see Oregon and Wisconsin.

Leo and Victoria at the Santa Monica pool after playing "Sharkie and Fishie."

Leo's first game at Fenway in April 2018.

John Linsley, my cousin Randy, Leo, me, and Randy's daughter Erica at Fenway in April 2018.

Watching the Boston Marathon, 2018.

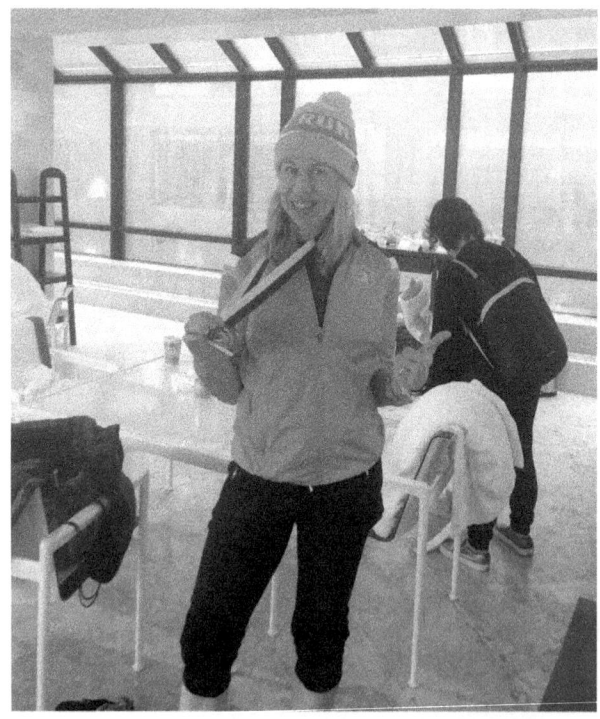

Susannah after completing the 2018 Boston Marathon.

Celebration dinner after Susie and Caesar's 2018 Boston Marathon.

Game 2 of the 2018 World Series with my cousin Randy at Fenway.

With my college roommates Marty Kaplan, Tom Werner, and Russell Goldsmith at Bartley's Burger Bar at our 45th Harvard College reunion in 2016.

Ryder Cup in Minneapolis, 2016.

Victoria, Leo, Susannah, and Janet at the Okoboji house in 2017.

With my siblings Scott Monk, Toni Brooks, and Tami Kuhl.

A family picture at Lake Okoboji, c. 2018.

Victoria and Leo at the driving range in Ojai, California, in 2018.

A 2018 family gathering in Ojai, with niece Hannah and her husband, Jeff Hartman, baby Pearl, James, Victoria, Janet, Leo, Caesar, and Susie.

With my aunt Jerenne in 2018.

With Janet at a Bruce Springsteen concert, the last show to be held at the Los Angeles Memorial Sports Arena before it was demolished.

Our black Lab, Homer, and yellow Lab, Marge, chilling in 2020 or so.

With friends Tom Meedel, Dennis Hickstein, and Jeff Greenberger in Okoboji in 2019.

Janet and her cousins Laura Kasser and Nancy Verstegen in Okoboji in 2019.

Victoria conducting her stuffed animal wedding in May of 2021.

An outing in 2021 to see the Dodgers with Caesar, Victoria, friend "Cappy," Leo, and Susie.

Cousin Randy's 70th birthday party at Buellton, California, in November 2021.

Our 2021 Thanksgiving dinner, set up to imitate the famous *Freedom From Want* painting by Norman Rockwell.

Birthday dinner for friend Tom Housel in December of 2021: Angela Light, Tom Housel, Janet, Caesar, Leo, Susie, me, Jon Light, and Victoria.

Leo and I with friends Jon Light and Tom Housel at SoFi Stadium in December 2021 to see the Rams versus Jacksonville.

Leo doing his happy dance after the Rams won the Super Bowl in 2022.

Susie and Victoria at my 73rd birthday dinner in Camarillo.

My Harvard suite mates at our 50th reunion: me, Jon Galassi, Steve Sicher, Russell Goldsmith, Tom Werner, and Marty Kaplan.

The gang is gathered at our house for the 2014 fantasy baseball draft. *From left*: Donna Johnsen, Bob Johnsen, David Bordeaux, Al Dowling, Jeff Kahn, Jon Light (holding trophy), Janet, with me above her, Vince Vignolle above me, Bruce Smart, Bill Creim, Tom Housel, Kathy Housel, and Joan Smart. In front are our Labs, Marge and Homer; Bruce's dog, Pepper Pickles; and Tom's dog, Fat Trapper.

MICHAEL W. MONK was born in Grand Island, Nebraska, and is a 1967 graduate of Grand Island Senior High School, the school to which he returned in 2015, metaphorically speaking, to contribute a bimonthly column for the alumni newsletter, collected here in *A Distant Mirror Anthology*. In 1971 Monk received his BA from Harvard College with a degree in English literature with honors. After graduating in 1974 from the University of Pennsylvania Law School, he practiced labor and employment law in Los Angeles for more than forty-six years. From 1990 to 1994, Monk was a minority owner of the San Diego Padres baseball team.

In 2014, Monk's play, *The Tragedy of Orenthal, Prince of Brentwood*, published by Small Batch Books, was named as a finalist in fiction for the Eric Hoffer Book Award and won an Outstanding Book of the Year award by the Independent Publisher Book Awards. Now mostly retired, Monk and his wife, Janet Bogle, reside a majority of the year at Lake Okoboji, Iowa.

www.ingramcontent.com/pod-product-compliance
Lightning Source LLC
Chambersburg PA
CBHW031620160426
43196CB00006B/218